SAVORY SWEET

simple preserves from a northern kitchen

beth dooley & mette nielsen

University of Minnesota Press

Minneapolis • London

The authors extend special gratitude to Abigail Wyckoff for photo styling.

Published by the University of Minnesota Press
111 Third Avenue South, Suite 290
Minneapolis, MN 55401-2520
http://www.upress.umn.edu

Book design by Brian Donahue and Jessica Collette / bedesign, inc.

Printed in Canada on acid-free paper

The University of Minnesota is an equal-opportunity educator and employer.

22 21 20 19 18 17   10 9 8 7 6 5 4 3 2 1

....

Library of Congress Cataloging-in-Publication Data
Dooley, Beth, author. | Nielsen, Mette, 1956– author.
Savory sweet : simple preserves from a northern kitchen / Beth Dooley and Mette Nielsen.
Minneapolis : University of Minnesota Press, [2017] | Includes index.
Identifiers: LCCN 2016046549 | ISBN 978-0-8166-9958-2 (hc)
Subjects: LCSH: Cooking, American–Midwestern style. | Cooking–Minnesota. | Canning and preserving. | LCGFT: Cookbooks.
Classification: LCC TX715.2.M53 D664 2017 | DDC 641.59776–dc23
LC record available at https://lccn.loc.gov/2016046549

To Abigail Wyckoff,
for making this book beautiful.
–METTE NIELSEN

....

To Kevin Dooley,
for his unwavering faith in my work.
–BETH DOOLEY

contents

SEASONINGS
Salty and Sweet

ACKNOWLEDGMENTS 196

INDEX 197

savory sweet

SIMPLE
PRESERVES
FROM A
NORTHERN
KITCHEN

L ET'S DISPENSE WITH THE USUAL OLD NOTIONS of preserving–that it's too hot, too messy, too complicated, too risky. Step into Mette Nielsen's kitchen, and learn a whole new way to create preserves. Photographer, master gardener, and intrepid cook, Mette grew up in Denmark and moved to Minneapolis in her early twenties after traveling the world. As she built her career and raised a son, she drew on her childhood memories to create a home filled with light, color, and great things to eat. She'll tell you that as a child she wasn't much interested in cooking and she really didn't care about food. But somehow, her dad's gardening, her mom's cooking, and their shared values around health and thrift must have sunk in. Caring for her young son, she paid attention to what she put on the table, grew her own, shopped the co-op and farmers markets, and cooked simple meals. That's also when she began to make condiments: chutneys, sauces, conserves, jams–jars of them for herself and friends. Here was a smart, delicious way to use up all those organic ingredients and add flavor and color to the most ordinary plate.

I've come to know Mette through our work on our cookbooks and newspaper articles. She brings to our partnership a knack for recognizing the inherent goodness–the color and flavor–in fresh ingredients. What must be embedded in her Nordic DNA is restraint. Paying attention to nature's tastes, she uses very little sugar in her creations and combines ingredients to contrast or complement each other for maximum punch. I've learned a great deal working in Mette's kitchen. Come into the kitchen, and we'll share these lessons with you.

Here's how to turn fresh produce at the peak of the season into brilliant condiments in no time flat–jams, chutneys, pickles, relishes, conserves, you name it. There's no long simmering, no tricky water baths; you don't have to sweat all day over a hot stove. Our recipes are practical and easy. They are inspired by the New Nordic Food manifesto calling for seasonal, healthy, and sustainable food. Because we live on the world's northern edges, where winter is cold and harsh but summer brings a luxury of long sunny days, we want to savor everything that comes from the earth. For a few short months, as our gardens are bursting and our farmers markets overflowing, we cooks try to keep all that's ripe from racing to rot. Here are recipes and methods to stock your kitchen with condiments you'll enjoy all year long.

The approach in these pages reflects Mette's Danish heritage, her sense of beauty, light, color, and bold tastes embedded in Nordic traditions. The cuisines of Norway, Sweden, Finland, Iceland, Greenland, Denmark, and the Faroe Islands are hyperlocal, minimalist, and practical. Today, these values play out in many kitchens in the world's northern regions, and they're so right for the way we live now.

Because growing conditions are at the root of any kitchen, our short season dictates that we make quick use of our harvest, waste nothing, and treat the earth's gifts with gratitude and respect. Governed by the weather, the light, and the land's fertility, we celebrate those first delicate asparagus and the brilliant tang of rhubarb; we lust for the musty goodness of August's corn. But we can't eat everything at once, so creating healthy condiments extends the season, gives that natural goodness another life. Using spices from the world's pantry—cardamom, ginger, coriander, cumin, hot peppers, and the traditional Nordic dill, caraway, and juniper—we pack a lot of flavor into small jars.

Mette is a gardener whose abundant garden more than meets her daily needs. I'm a farmers market shopper, forever lugging home more than my family can possibly eat. We cook from different perspectives, yet share a desire to preserve summer's bounty. Together, Mette and I have fashioned sensible recipes that are low-tech, easy, and quick. They yield small quantities, and the cooking times are short, so the focus is on fresh tastes. We do not attempt to make these products shelf stable by processing the jars in hot water because that overcooks the food. Instead, we rely on the refrigerator and freezer for storage. Our methods retain the foods' bright, fresh colors and flavors—sweet and sour, hot and mellow.

Our recipes are forgiving and flexible. We hope you'll make substitutions based on your own tastes and what you have on hand. Like our grandmothers, we don't rely on scientific accuracy and our methods may seem imprecise, but there's joy in this more relaxed and intuitive approach. Using a few basic techniques, it's easy to improvise. Consider these recipes mere guidelines to creating a kitchen arsenal. With a well-stocked refrigerator and freezer, you're always ready for that last-minute guest.

PRESERVING 2.0

Let's redefine the term *preserving* to connote transformation. We are not putting food up to rely on through the winter or to stock the shelves for survival. Those days are long gone. Instead, we are preserving to keep this precious, beautiful food from hitting the compost pile. True to our Nordic values, we're making use of every delicious tomato, all the beans, and every squash—no waste, great taste. We're not really "preserving," which makes perishable food shelf stable. These small-batch products are to be stored in the refrigerator or freezer, ready to be enjoyed at any time. They're essential components in a contemporary kitchen, handy tools for enlivening colors and flavors on the simplest of plates.

THE NEW NORTHERN APPROACH

You won't need anything fancy to make these easy preserves. The techniques are simple.

Organized by ingredient: Did you pick too many blueberries or fill a crate with apples from your favorite orchard? Organized by vegetable and fruit rather than preserving method (e.g., jelly, pickle), the short chapters focus on specific ingredients.

Small batch: Small batches are great for small kitchens. Plus, working with small quantities means shorter cooking times and less mess. Less time on the stove yields a fresher-tasting product.

No tricky preserving methods, everyday equipment: Store these preserves in the refrigerator and freezer, not your pantry. Reuse the jars and lids again and again.

No artificial ingredients: With no added pectin, stabilizers, or artificial colors in these recipes, you know what you're getting.

Little sugar, big taste: Traditional recipes often call for a lot of sugar. We've cut the sugar by more than half, so the true flavors shine through.

Healthy preserved foods: When cooked quickly (and not overcooked in a canning water bath), fresh fruits and vegetables retain their nutrients.

Bright, interesting flavors: Be surprised by the range of savory and sweet, spicy and tart flavors in these preserved foods. They brighten ordinary meals and make homespun, heartfelt gifts.

Year round: No need to put everything up at once. Find tips for using frozen produce, storage vegetables, dried fruits, and nuts that are available all year long.

Quick ideas: Once you make them, use them up! Each recipe includes tips and hints for enjoying these preserved foods ASAP.

Defining cuts: minced, 1/16- to 1/8-inch pieces *(top left)*; finely diced, 1/8- to 1/4-inch pieces *(top right)*; medium diced, 1/4- to 3/8-inch pieces *(bottom left)*; coarsely chopped, 1/2- to 3/4-inch pieces *(bottom right)*.

No fancy equipment needed!

THE TOOLS

You probably already have these in your kitchen.

Bowls: Stainless steel or glass bowls are best. Avoid plastic, as it tends to discolor and scratches easily, leaving bits of plastic in the food. Enamel and ceramic bowls, if old and worn, may crack, and the glaze may flake into the food.

Pots: Heavy, stainless steel pots are best. Reactive cookware, such as aluminum and cast iron, reacts with acidic ingredients, giving them an off flavor and appearance. A good four-quart stockpot and small and medium saucepans are what we rely on.

10-inch sauté pan with a lid: A high-sided, heavy-bottomed stainless steel pan with a lid is a must. The heavier the bottom, the more evenly ingredients will cook and the less likely they will be to stick and scorch. We use this pan for just about all of our recipes, sweet and savory.

While cast iron is great for roasting vegetables and searing meat, it is heavy and difficult to clean. Nonstick pans, when older and worn, may flake into the food.

Foil, wax paper, and parchment: These products serve a variety of purposes. The wax paper, cut into small squares and placed in the top of the jar, will help keep the ingredients submerged in the brine as the liquid rises to cover the paper.

Use aluminum foil or parchment for easy clean-up when roasting vegetables. Line baking sheets with parchment for temperatures under 425 degrees and with aluminum foil for anything hotter. When roasting on the stovetop, line a frying pan with foil to create a "nonstick" surface. Use the corners of the foil to lift the vegetables out.

Measuring cups, measuring spoons, sieves: For dry ingredients, use stainless steel measuring cups. Dip the measuring cup into the ingredient, and then level it off with a knife. Stainless steel measuring spoons and sieves are the most durable and the easiest to clean.

Use glass measuring cups for liquids because you can see the contents. The spout makes it easy to pour the liquid.

Cut squares of wax paper slightly larger than the jar opening. With a spoon, push a square of wax paper under the brine. Bend in the corners so the product is covered with the paper and a little liquid seeps over the top.

Scale: A small digital scale comes in handy when working with fresh produce that varies greatly in size and yield (e.g., the weight of a quart of strawberries may fluctuate depending on how big and juicy the berries are). We give measurements in weight and cups.

Spoons and spatulas: A long stainless steel or wooden spoon is necessary for reaching into deep pots; use smaller spoons for filling jars. The advantage of a wooden spoon is that it won't scratch the pot and doesn't conduct heat. Stainless steel spatulas and spoons are the easiest to clean.

Jars: We use a variety of straight-sided mason jars with two-part lids. That way we always have the option of storing the jars in the freezer.

Defining zests: (*top left*) finely grated zest (fine grater); (*top right*) finely grated ginger (fine grater); (*bottom left*) wide bands of zest (vegetable peeler or paring knife); (*bottom right*) coarsely grated ginger (coarse side of box grater).

Cutting boards: Use a good, heavy plastic or wood cutting board.

Knives: A ten-inch French knife and a paring knife are enough to get the job done.

Peeler: A vegetable peeler is essential.

Funnel: A wide-mouth funnel is helpful for filling jars while keeping the rims clean.

THE TECHNIQUES

Prep and measure: Things can go quickly when you're preserving, so prep and measure your ingredients before you begin. Chefs call this *mise en place*, or "put into place." Measure out spices into small bowls or fill spice bags ahead of time.

Reduce by half (aka the dipstick method): Here's a quick tip. Insert the handle of a wooden spoon or a skewer into the liquid to be reduced, holding it straight up and down and making sure it touches the bottom. Remove, and mark the "wet line" with a pencil. As the liquid cooks and reduces, insert the skewer or handle into the liquid again and note the new wet line. This will indicate how much the liquid has been reduced.

Measure liquid reduction by placing a wooden tool (dipstick) in the pot; mark the top of the wet line. As the liquid cooks and evaporates, note the amount of reduction.

How thick is "thick"? None of these recipes call for added pectin, the commercial product that helps jellies and jams jell; instead, we rely on the fruit's natural pectin and add small amounts of acid (citrus or vinegar), which reacts with sugar to set the preserve. We simmer the preserves gently to reduce the liquid until they're pleasantly thick.

To test for doneness, put a small plate in the freezer as you begin the recipe. When the cooked preserve seems nearly ready, put a spoonful on the frozen plate and return it to the freezer for about two minutes. Drag your finger through the center. If the mark doesn't fill back in, the cooked preserve is ready to spoon into jars; if it seems runny, return the pan to the stove and cook a few more minutes; then repeat the test. Generally, it's better to undercook than to overcook a preserve. (You can always return it to the stove, but you can't uncook it.) Our methods are not scientific. We also know that no two stoves are alike and fresh ingredients are inconsistent. The best technique is to rely on your senses.

Set test: Place some cooked preserve on a cold plate or a baking sheet and put it in the freezer for two minutes. Run your finger through the chilled preserve: if it doesn't run together, it's set.

Cleaning and filling jars: Use canning jars with lids and bands, and carefully clean them before you fill the jars. We don't sterilize jars and lids in boiling water, as is often called for in preserving recipes. Sterilizing is an essential step if the product is to be shelf stable. For these recipes, simply washing the jars, lids, and bands is sufficient.

1. Wash the jars, lids, and bands in very hot soapy water and rinse well. Place the jars, lids, and bands upside down on a clean towel to drain.

2. To fill, turn the jars over and add the food.

3. Leave about a half inch of headroom to allow the contents to expand when freezing.

4. Wipe the rims with a clean wet cloth or paper towel; add the lids and bands, and finger tighten the bands.

5. Alternately, rinse the jars with vodka or any hard (no sugar added) liquor before adding the preserves. (Note: This method is **not** advised by the USDA.)

6. Label and date the jars.

Create a system for labeling jars, such as using a different label color for each month.

A word about composting: We recommend composting produce waste. Composting keeps fruit and vegetable peels, seeds, and the like out of our landfills and garbage burners. Here's a general rule of thumb: If the fruits and vegetables are uncooked, they go into the backyard compost. If they're cooked and contain spices, sugar, or oil, then put them into the city or county compost.

Organic? No debate here. We use organic produce for a lot of reasons. It's loaded with nutrients, not chemicals, and it's grown responsibly to protect the soil, water, and wildlife. If, however, your local farmer uses organic practices but isn't certified organic, and you trust that he or she using best practices—rotating crops, avoiding chemicals—then choose that produce too.

THE GOOD STUFF

Herbs: For the best flavor in our recipes, we call for fresh herbs. They're readily available throughout the year in co-ops and grocery stores.

Spices: Buy bulk spices so you can get only the amount you need. Spices are expensive and, while they last longer than dried herbs, they can lose their punch. The flavor and heat levels will vary depending on the age and source of the spice. (Taste as you cook.) Some recipes call for spice bags. Here are some options:

Spice bags keep loose spices from dispersing through the preserve. Spice bags are available online, in cookware stores, and in some groceries, co-ops, and supermarkets.

Spice balls, which look like big tea infusers, are available in kitchen stores and online.

Disposable tea filters work well but can be fragile. Use these when there's little stirring and the bag simply nestles in the food as it simmers. Once filled, secure the filter with a toothpick.

Cheesecloth bags are a cinch to make. Cut a square of cheesecloth, and put the spices in the center. Tie the bag together with a bit of string or a strip of cheesecloth.

Salt: Sea salt is the best-tasting choice for preserving. Kosher salt is good too. The salinity of sea salts can vary, so start with a light hand and taste as you go. Do not use salt that contains anti-caking agents or iodine, as they discolor fruits and vegetables in a pickle. We don't work with pickling salt. If you do, use smaller amounts than called for in these recipes: pickling salt has a finer texture than other salts, so more grains fit in a measuring spoon.

Sugar: We prefer evaporated cane sugar because it's less processed than beet sugar. It carries the slightest hint of molasses flavor. The grains are a little bigger than those of beet sugar, but it performs the same. Light brown sugar is called for in several recipes for its subtle molasses notes. Avoid dark brown sugar: the flavor can overwhelm.

Vinegar—the acidic essence: Apple cider vinegar is our kitchen workhorse. We rely on unfiltered, unpasteurized, organic apple cider vinegar. It is acidic enough to brine and pickle foods, yet it has a slightly sweet finish. It's less harsh than simple white vinegar. We also call for a variety of other vinegars for color and flavor.

Making preserves builds a kitchen arsenal of delicious and dependable ingredients necessary to being a spontaneous, seasonal cook.

Buy bulk spices. Store them in four-ounce glass jars that are labeled and kept out of direct sunlight.

vegetables

METTE IS ALWAYS IN A PICKLE—savory, spicy, or sweet. These boldly seasoned condiments provide a pleasing contrast and piquancy to the simplest foods. They'll transform a slice of roast turkey and a hunk of bread into lunch, turn a cheese plate into an elegant hors d'oeuvre, brighten a pale potato soup. Mette is one of the most frugal cooks I know, and creating condiments from the vegetables she grows and finds at the farmers market appeals to her Nordic sense of frugality. After months of gardening or even a morning of shopping the farmers market, neither of us ever wants to waste a single scrap of good local produce. There's joy, of course, in eating seasonally, devouring the day's harvest at dinner that night, but there's also real pleasure in preserving the moment in a jar—a cook's snapshot of plenty.

The work is immensely satisfying. We chop and simmer, steaming up the kitchen with comforting, spicy aromas. These condiments all make great eating and wonderful gifts.

LEXICON OF CONDIMENTS

The meanings of these terms vary from cook to cook. Here's how we define them:

Chutneys are most often cooked a little longer, and their flavors are more complex.

Relishes have fewer spices and tend to be a little lighter, their flavors more straightforward.

Pickles are usually brined in a salty solution with vinegar, and sometimes a little sugar, and seasoned with herbs and spices. Pickled foods are raw or lightly cooked.

Keep the vegetables the same size. Cut the vegetables into pieces roughly the same size so they cook evenly.

Testing for doneness. These recipes are not scientific, so use your best judgment to determine if a product is ready to jar. The consistency tends to become firmer as the condiments cool. A chutney is done when you can drag a large spoon across the pan and the mixture holds its shape.

Create your own recipes. Once you master the ratios of vinegar to sugar, you can vary the recipes to your own taste. That's the charm. Use chopped apricots instead of dried cranberries, diced parsnips for carrots or beets, a pinch of chili flakes, horseradish instead of ginger—you get the idea.

asparagus

The first crop of the season! Choose the thinnest, tallest, finest, freshest asparagus that appear in early spring. They make fabulous pickles you'll enjoy long after the short season is over.

pickled asparagus with juniper and fennel

MAKES 3 PINTS

Unlike most recipes for pickled asparagus, this one does not call for blanching the stalks before brining, so they retain their snap and fresh flavors. Note that the color will change from vibrant green to olive. The juniper adds a nuanced peppery-piney note, while a little fennel seed gives a licorice scent.

Seek out two tall 24-ounce jars to hold the stalks upright; otherwise, standard wide-mouth pint jars will work. You can eat the leftover trimmed stalks for your next meal.

Wait at least a week before enjoying this pickle to allow the flavors to marry. The jars will keep several months in the refrigerator.

VEGETABLES
- 1 to 1¼ pounds asparagus
- 4 large garlic cloves, quartered lengthwise
- 2 teaspoons juniper berries
- 1 teaspoon fennel seeds
- 1 teaspoon black peppercorns
- 1 teaspoon coriander seeds
- 1 teaspoon crushed red pepper flakes

BRINE
- 1¾ cups water
- 1¾ cups cider vinegar
- 2 tablespoons sugar
- 1 teaspoon salt

Wash and trim the asparagus to fit in your jars, allowing for a half inch of headspace.

Wash the jars, lids, and bands in very hot soapy water, rinse them well, and place them upside down on a clean towel to drain.

Divide the asparagus between the jars. (We like putting the tips up.) Distribute the garlic, juniper berries, fennel seeds, peppercorns, coriander seeds, and crushed red pepper flakes among the jars.

Combine the water, vinegar, sugar, and salt in a small saucepan, and bring it to a boil. Stir to dissolve the sugar and salt. Pour the hot brine over the asparagus.

Cover each jar with a square of wax paper slightly larger than the jar opening, fold in the corners with a clean spoon, and push down lightly so some of the brine comes up over the wax paper. Wipe the rims with a clean wet cloth or paper towel, add the lids and bands, and finger tighten the bands.

Label the jars. Cool completely and tighten the bands before storing in the refrigerator.

QUICK IDEAS // These tall, delicious spears make an edible stir stick for classic cocktails like Bloody Marys and Gibsons. The pickle's light juniper flavor pairs nicely with both vodka and gin. This pickle is also delicious layered into a grilled cheese or ham and cheese sandwich. Substitute pickled asparagus for the green beans in a niçoise salad, and whisk a little of the pickle brine into the vinaigrette.

beans

Beans, beans, beans. They come galloping into our gardens and markets faster than we can pick them. We use both fresh and dried beans. If you can, find freshly dried local beans at the farmers market. They have more flavor and are more tender.

white bean dip with oven-dried tomatoes and smoked paprika

MAKES 4 TO 5 HALF-PINTS

Smoked paprika gives this lush dip its rose color and hint of smoke. The recipe calls for cooked dried beans, but if you're in a hurry, substitute well-rinsed canned organic beans. This dip freezes beautifully.

1 cup (7 ounces) dried white beans or 3 cups cooked or canned beans, rinsed well

3 bay leaves

⅓ cup olive oil, plus more if needed

1 cup medium-diced onion

2 tablespoons minced garlic

1 cup medium-diced oven-dried tomatoes (page 79) or sun-dried tomatoes

½ cup water (bean cooking water or tap water if using canned beans)

2 tablespoons cider vinegar

1 tablespoon sweet smoked paprika

2 teaspoons salt

10 to 15 grinds black pepper

Soak the dried beans in cold water for at least 8 hours, changing the water a couple of times. Drain the beans and put them and the bay leaves into a large pot with enough cold fresh water to cover the beans by about 4 inches. Set the pot over high heat, bring the liquid to a boil, reduce the heat to simmer, and cook until the beans are tender, about 1 hour. Drain the beans, reserving about 1 cup of the cooking water. Discard the bay leaves.

Put 2 tablespoons of the olive oil and the onions and garlic into a 10-inch sauté pan, and set it over medium-low heat. Cook, stirring often, until soft and translucent, about 5 minutes. Be careful the onions and garlic do not brown. Stir in the oven-dried tomatoes, and cook another 5 minutes.

Transfer the onion mixture to a food processor, and pulse a few times. Add the beans, remaining olive oil, ½ cup of reserved cooking water, vinegar, paprika, salt, and pepper. Process the mixture, pausing occasionally to scrape down the sides. Taste, and adjust the seasoning. If the mixture is too thick, add a little more oil or bean water.

Wash the jars, lids, and bands in very hot soapy water, rinse them well, and place them upside down on a clean towel to drain.

Spoon the bean dip into the jars, leaving a half inch of headroom to allow for expansion during freezing. Wipe the rims with a clean wet cloth or paper towel, add the lids and bands, and finger tighten the bands.

Label the jars. Cool completely, and tighten the bands before storing in refrigerator or freezer.

QUICK IDEAS // Use this dip as a spread for veggie sandwiches of sliced tomatoes and sprouts and thick-sliced whole wheat bread. Stuff it into pita pockets along with sliced cucumbers. Slather it on tacos and nachos.

spicy wax beans with tarragon

MAKES 2 PINTS

The beans are not blanched in this recipe, so it's important to trim both ends to ensure they soak up the brine. Use fresh, not dried, tarragon for its taste and contrasting color.

VEGETABLES

¾ pound tender, straight yellow waxbeans, ends trimmed

4 large sprigs tarragon

BRINE

1½ cups cider vinegar

¾ cup water

2 tablespoons sugar

2 teaspoons salt

1 teaspoon black peppercorns

1 teaspoon coriander seeds

1 teaspoon crushed red pepper flakes

½ teaspoon whole allspice

Wash the jars, lids, and bands in very hot soapy water, rinse them well, and place them upside down on a clean towel to drain.

Wash and trim the beans, and pat them dry in a clean towel. Divide the beans and the tarragon sprigs among the jars.

Combine the vinegar, water, sugar, salt, peppercorns, coriander, crushed red pepper flakes, and allspice in a small saucepan set over medium heat, and bring the brine to a gentle boil. Stir to dissolve the sugar and salt. Pour the hot brine over the beans.

Cover each jar with a square of wax paper slightly larger than the jar opening, fold in the corners with a clean spoon, and push down gently so some of the brine comes up over the wax paper. Wipe the rims with a clean wet cloth or paper towel, add the lids and bands, and finger tighten the bands.

Label the jars. Cool completely and tighten the bands before storing the jars in the refrigerator.

QUICK IDEAS // Use these beans as a garnish for warm or cold tomato soup or smoked trout or salmon. Cut the beans in pieces and toss them into a panzanella salad made with tart, sweet cherry tomatoes and plenty of mozzarella, and whisk the pickle brine into the vinaigrette.

beets

Nordic palates prefer beets to be pickled. No wonder, the flavors of this sweet, earthy vegetable shine with a kiss of vinegar and herbs. Red and golden beets are interchangeable in all of these recipes. Be careful when working with red beets—they stain everything they touch. Yellow beets tend to be sweeter and have a more delicate flavor.

pickled golden beets with chili and grapefruit

MAKES 3 HALF-PINTS

Golden beets make a very pretty pickle. Be patient: it takes about a week for the spices to marry. The longer you wait, the better these beets will taste.

VEGETABLES
- 1 pound golden beets, scrubbed
- 2 teaspoons salt
- 6 wide bands grapefruit zest
- 1 fresh red Fresno chili or other hot chili, seeded and cut into thin strips
- 3 bay leaves

SPICE MIX
- 1 teaspoon yellow mustard seeds
- 1 teaspoon brown mustard seeds
- 1 teaspoon coriander seeds
- 1 teaspoon cardamom seeds, slightly crushed
- 1 teaspoon fennel seeds
- 1 teaspoon juniper berries

BRINE
- ½ cup water
- ½ cup cider vinegar
- 1½ tablespoons sugar
- 2 tablespoons fresh grapefruit juice

Wash the jars, lids, and bands in very hot soapy water, rinse them well, and place them upside down on a clean towel to drain.

Place the beets in a medium saucepan with the salt, and add enough water to cover by about 2 inches. Set the pan over high heat, and bring the water to a boil. Reduce the heat to a simmer, cover, and cook the beets until a sharp knife slides easily into the center, about 20 to 30 minutes, depending on size. (Take care not to overcook the beets. Remove them from the pot as they are done.) Drain and refresh the cooked beets in cold water. When the beets are cool enough to handle, slip off the skins using your fingers or a sharp knife. Cut the beets lengthwise into thin wedges. In a small bowl, stir together the mustard seeds, coriander, cardamom, fennel, and juniper berries.

Divide the beets, grapefruit zest, pepper strips, bay leaves, and spice mix among the jars.

continued on next page

In a saucepan, stir together the water, vinegar, sugar, and grapefruit juice, and set the pan over high heat. Bring the brine to a boil, and stir to dissolve the sugar. Remove from the heat.

Pour the brine over the beets. Cover each jar with a square of wax paper slightly larger than the jar opening, fold in the corners with a clean spoon, and push down gently so some of the brine comes up over the wax paper. Wipe the rims with a clean wet cloth or paper towel, add the lids and bands, and finger tighten the bands.

Label the jars. Cool the jars completely and tighten the bands before storing in the refrigerator. Allow at least 3 days for the flavors to marry before eating. These beets get better with time.

QUICK IDEAS // Serve the beets in a composed salad on arugula or spring greens with crumbled chèvre. Whisk together equal parts brine and walnut oil or olive oil to make a tangy vinaigrette to drizzle over the salad.

roasted beet and tomato relish

MAKES ABOUT 4 HALF-PINTS

In this nicely balanced relish, the sweet, earthy flavor of the beets shines through. We use mild rice vinegar and a little balsamic vinegar for depth of flavor.

1½ pounds red beets

 2 tablespoons olive oil

 ¼ cup sugar

 ⅓ cup rice vinegar

 2 tablespoons balsamic vinegar

 ¾ cup finely diced red onion

 2 tablespoons prepared horseradish or freshly grated horseradish

 ½ cup tomato puree

 1 teaspoon salt

10 to 15 grinds black pepper

Preheat the oven to 350 degrees. Wash and trim the beets, place them in a roasting pan, and drizzle them with the olive oil. Put the pan in the middle of the oven, and roast the beets for about 1 hour, depending on size. Check for doneness after 45 minutes: a knife will slide easily into the center of a cooked beet. Remove any cooked beets from the pan before returning the others to the oven.

When the beets are cool enough to handle, slip off the skins using your fingers or a sharp knife. Coarsely grate or finely dice the beets: you should have about 2 cups. Set the beets aside.

Combine the sugar, vinegars, onion, and horseradish in a 10-inch sauté pan set over medium-high heat. Bring the mixture to a gentle boil; then reduce the heat and simmer for 5 minutes. Add the tomato puree, and simmer for another minute or two. Add the grated beets, and continue simmering until the mixture thickens, about 10 minutes. Taste the relish, and season it with salt and pepper.

Wash the jars, lids, and bands in very hot soapy water, rinse them well, and place them upside down on a clean towel to drain.

Spoon the relish into the jars, leaving a half inch of headroom to allow for expansion during freezing. Wipe the rims with a clean wet cloth or paper towel, add the lids and bands, and finger tighten the bands.

Label the jars. Cool completely and tighten the bands before storing in the refrigerator or freezer.

QUICK IDEAS // This condiment is wonderful with smoked and cured meats, strong cheeses, and pickled, smoked, and grilled fish. Swirl in a little mayonnaise, and put a dollop on a burger or toss it into a smoked chicken salad.

broccoli and cauliflower

When it comes to pickling, broccoli, cauliflower, Romanesco (a relative of cauliflower), and Broccolini can all be treated the same way. Use a mix of color and shapes in either of these recipes. Put those stems to delicious use.

pickled broccoli with indian spices

MAKES 3 PINTS

Black mustard seeds are kickier than the more familiar brown seeds. Find them in Indian markets or online. Brown mustard seeds will also work in this recipe if you increase the amount a little or opt for a slightly less spicy pickle.

VEGETABLES
- 1 pound broccoli, florets cut and stems peeled and sliced (about 6 cups)
- 2 tablespoons minced garlic
- 2 tablespoons minced fresh ginger
- 1 tablespoon black mustard seeds
- 2 teaspoons crushed red pepper flakes
- 1 tablespoon sunflower oil or other neutral oil

BRINE
- 1½ cups malt vinegar
- 1½ cups water
- 3 tablespoons sugar
- 1 teaspoon salt

In a large bowl, toss together the broccoli, garlic, ginger, mustard seeds, crushed red pepper flakes, and oil, using your hands to be sure it's thoroughly mixed.

Wash the jars, lids, and bands in very hot soapy water, rinse them well, and place them upside down on a clean towel to drain. Turn jars over, and add the broccoli mixture.

In a medium saucepan, whisk together the vinegar, water, sugar, and salt. Heat just until the sugar and salt have dissolved. Pour the hot vinegar mixture into the jars, leaving about a half inch of headroom.

Cover each jar with a square of wax paper slightly larger than the jar opening, fold in the corners with a clean spoon, and gently push down so some of the brine comes up over the wax paper. Wipe the rims with a clean wet cloth or paper towel, add the lids and bands, and finger tighten the bands.

Label the jars. Let the jars rest in the refrigerator for a couple of weeks before eating so the flavors marry. This pickle will store nicely for several months.

QUICK IDEAS // Pack these pickles for a picnic, or in a lunch box. They're terrific with deviled eggs and cheese sandwiches and great as a quick, light nibble when guests arrive.

spicy pickled vegetables

MAKES 3 TO 4 PINTS

Here's an updated twist on traditional piccalilli, the classic British mix of vegetables in yellow mustard sauce; This recipe is bit spicier and brighter thanks to the addition of paprika and cayenne.

Let your imagination and whatever looks fresh guide your choice of vegetables. Just remember to use about 2 pounds of vegetables, or about 8 to 9 cups of cut vegetables.

VEGETABLES

- 6 cups water
- ½ cup salt
- 1½ cups coarsely chopped carrots (about ½ pound)
- 2 cups coarsely chopped celeriac (about ½ pound)
- 2 cups coarsely chopped onions (about ½ pound)
- 3 cups small cauliflower florets (about ½ pound)

SAUCE

- 2 cups cider vinegar
- ½ cup sugar
- 2 teaspoons sweet Hungarian paprika
- 2 teaspoons curry powder
- 2 teaspoons English mustard powder
- 2 teaspoons ground turmeric
- 1 teaspoon cayenne pepper
- 2 tablespoons cornstarch, stirred into a little cold water (optional)

In a large bowl, whisk together the water and the salt. As you cut the vegetables, drop them into the salt brine. Mix well, and cover. Leave the covered bowl on the kitchen counter, out of direct sunlight, for 12 hours.

Drain the vegetables in a colander, and rinse them well under cold running water. Fill a bowl with ice water. Set a large pot of water over high heat, and bring the water to a boil. Blanch the vegetables until they are just tender-crisp, about 3 to 4 minutes, being careful they don't overcook. Drain the vegetables, and turn them into the ice water to shock them until cold. Drain the vegetables, and turn them into a large bowl.

In a medium saucepan, combine the vinegar, sugar, paprika, curry powder, mustard powder, turmeric, and cayenne. Set the pan over medium-low heat, and bring to a gentle boil. Whisk well to dissolve the sugar and incorporate the spices; then reduce the heat and simmer about 5 minutes to blend the flavors. If using the cornstarch, whisk it in a little at a time to slightly thicken the sauce. Pour the sauce over the vegetables, and toss to coat.

Wash the jars, lids, and bands in very hot soapy water, rinse them well, and place them upside down on a clean towel to drain.

Divide the vegetables among the jars. Press down to make the vegetables fit, if necessary. Leave a half inch of headroom in each jar. Cover each jar with a square of wax paper slightly larger than the jar opening, fold in the corners with a clean spoon, and gently push so some of the sauce comes up over the wax paper. Wipe the rims with a clean wet cloth or paper towel, add the lids and bands, and finger tighten the bands.

Label the jars. Cool completely, and tighten the bands before storing in the refrigerator. Let the pickled vegetables rest for a few days before eating so the flavors marry. These will store nicely for several months.

QUICK IDEAS // This condiment is great on hot dogs, bratwurst, hamburgers, sausages, eggs and toast, cheeses, and sliced cold meats such as roast beef, smoked turkey, and ham.

cabbage

In Nordic countries, every cook has a special recipe for pickled cabbage; these recipes are some of Mette's favorites. We intentionally undercook the ingredients to maintain the distinctive crunch.

crunchy pickled red cabbage with jalapeño

MAKES ABOUT 4 PINTS

In true Danish tradition, Mette's family prepares pickled red cabbage in time for the holiday feasts. It's served warm or at room temperature. In this version, jalapeños add a little heat. (Leave the seeds in the peppers for more kick.) No need to wait for Christmas—this cabbage is delicious any time of year.

VEGETABLES

- 2 pounds red cabbage
- ¼ cup minced jalapeño pepper
- 3 tablespoons salt

BRINE

- 2 cups red wine vinegar
- 1 cup cider vinegar
- 1 cup water
- ¾ cup sugar
- 1 tablespoon black peppercorns
- 1 tablespoon juniper berries
- 1 tablespoon coriander seeds
- 4 bay leaves

Wash the cabbage well, and remove the outer leaves. Quarter the head, and remove the hard core. Using a sharp knife, cut the quarters into very thin slices. You should have 10 cups.

In a large bowl, toss the cabbage with the jalapeños and salt, using your hands to be sure everything is thoroughly mixed. Cover the bowl, and leave it on the kitchen counter, out of direct sunlight, for 24 hours. The cabbage may turn slightly blue at this stage.

Turn the cabbage and peppers into a colander, and rinse well under cold running water. Set the cabbage aside to drain.

Combine the vinegars, water, sugar, peppercorns, juniper berries, coriander, and bay leaves in a medium sauce pan set over medium heat. Bring the brine to a gentle boil, and stir to dissolve the sugar. Turn off the heat, cover, and let the brine rest for 1 hour to allow the brine to take on the flavors of the spices.

Wash the jars, lids, and bands in very hot soapy water, rinse them well, and place them upside down on a clean towel to drain. Turn the jars over, and divide the red cabbage among the jars, pressing down so that it fits, and leaving a half inch of headroom.

Set the pan of brine over medium-high heat, and bring the brine back up to a boil. Strain the brine into a large measuring cup, and discard the spices.

Pour or ladle the brine over the red cabbage. Cover each jar with a square of wax paper slightly larger than the jar opening, fold in the corners with a clean spoon, and gently push down so some of the brine comes up over the wax paper. Wipe the rims with a clean wet cloth or paper towel, add the lids and bands, and finger tighten the bands.

Label the jars. Cool completely, and tighten the bands before storing the jars in the refrigerator. Allow the cabbage to rest for a few days before eating so the spices marry. The longer the cabbage rests, the better it will taste.

QUICK IDEAS // This is great on grilled sausages and bratwurst, roast pork, and lamb. Pile the cabbage onto a Reuben or pastrami and rye sandwich. Serve it as a side to pierogi and shepherd's pie.

simple kraut with apples and coriander

MAKES 2 QUARTS

There's nothing complicated about this kind of fermentation: all you need is patience and time, about 7 to 9 weeks (give or take).

Use the old-fashioned clip-top preserving jars with rubber gaskets that seal the jars: the gaskets keep oxygen out while allowing some of the gases and liquid to escape. While it may seem like a long time until the cabbage is ready, your patience will be rewarded with its wonderful taste.

1½ tablespoons coriander seeds

1 tablespoon salt

2 pounds red or green cabbage

½ pound tart apples

4 cups water, boiled and cooled

Rinse one 2-quart or two 1-quart clip-top preserving jars and gaskets with boiling water.

In a small bowl, mix the coriander seeds and the salt.

Reserve 2 large cabbage leaves to place on top of the jars later. Cut the cabbage in half, and slice it as thin as possible. Remove the stem and flower from the apples. Cut the apples in half and then in thin wedges, leaving the core and seeds in place. You should have about 2 cups of apple wedges.

Fill the jars, layering the cabbage, the apples, and the coriander mixture. After adding each layer, press down hard using a wooden muddler, a wooden spoon, or your fist until liquid seeps up from the bottom. Keep adding more layers, pressing down very hard after each layer is added.

Fill the jars to 1¼ inch from the top with the cooled boiled water so the vegetables are completely covered by water. Place a reserved cabbage leaf on top of each jar, and press down until liquid comes up over the top.

Seal the jars, place them on a plate to catch any liquid that seeps from the jars, and store at room temperature, out of direct sunlight, for 2 to 3 days. Then move the jars to a slightly cooler spot, about 60 degrees, for 2 to 3 weeks. Then move the jars to the refrigerator for another 4 to 6 weeks, when the kraut will finally be ready to eat. The longer you wait, the better this kraut will taste.

QUICK IDEAS // Enjoy this kraut as you would sauerkraut—on bratwurst, grilled or smoked pork, Reuben sandwiches, and corned beef. It's great with fried fish and roast chicken, too.

carrots

Carrots work beautifully in sweet recipes as well as in savory preserves. Because good-quality carrots are available all year round, there's no rush to preserve them in the peak of the season. These are good recipes to make on a dreary winter afternoon.

danish pickled carrots

MAKES 2 PINTS

Mette's father loved caraway seeds, especially sprinkled over open-faced sandwiches. Caraway, dill, and bay are the holy trinity of Danish seasoning; in this pickle, the whole is far greater than each spice.

BRINE
- 1 cup cider vinegar
- ½ cup water
- 2 tablespoons sugar
- 1 teaspoon salt
- 1 teaspoon dill seeds
- 1 teaspoon caraway seeds
- 1 teaspoon black peppercorns

VEGETABLES
- 1 pound carrots, sliced ¼ inch thick (3½ cups)
- 4 bay leaves

Wash the jars, lids, and bands in very hot soapy water, rinse them well, and place them upside down on a clean towel to drain. Turn the jars over, and layer the carrots and bay leaves into the jars, tightly packing them down.

Combine the vinegar, water, sugar, salt, dill seed, caraway seed, and peppercorns in a small saucepan set over medium heat, and bring to a gentle boil. Stir until the sugar dissolves. Remove the pan from the heat, and pour or ladle the brine into the jars.

Cover each jar with a square of wax paper slightly larger than the jar opening, fold in the corners with a clean spoon, and gently push down so some of the brine comes up over the wax paper. Wipe the rims with a clean wet cloth or paper towel, add the lids and bands, and finger tighten the bands.

Label the jars. Cool completely, tighten the bands, and store in the refrigerator. Allow the jars to rest in the refrigerator for at least 2 weeks so the flavors marry.

QUICK IDEAS // These carrots are the ultimate garnish to an appetizer platter of rich cheeses, cured meats, pâtés, and artisan crackers. Try these pickles with roast chicken or pork.

carrot lemon marmalade with ginger and cardamom

MAKES 3 TO 4 HALF-PINTS

Storage carrots, a variety that sweetens after being stored, are released around the holidays. They're especially good in this fragrant marmalade.

½ pound lemons

1 pound carrots, peeled

2 cups water

¾ cup sugar

1 tablespoon finely grated fresh ginger

1 teaspoon ground cardamom

Scrub the lemons well under running water, and remove the hard blossom ends and any blemishes on the skin. Cut the fruit in half lengthwise, and place it cut side down on a cutting board. Slice the lemon halves into very thin slices, discarding the seeds; you should have about 2 cups.

Using either a box grater or a food processor, coarsely grate the carrots. You should have about 3½ loosely packed cups of grated carrots.

Put the lemons, carrots, and water into a 10-inch sauté pan. Cover the pan, and let it sit at room temperature, out of direct sunlight, for at least 8 to 24 hours to soften the lemon peel.

Put a small plate in the freezer for the set test. Stir the sugar, ginger, and cardamom into the carrot mixture. Set the pan over medium heat, and bring it to a gentle boil. Reduce the heat and simmer, uncovered, stirring occasionally, until most of the liquid has evaporated, about 45 to 50 minutes. The marmalade should be sticky and slightly thickened. Remove the pan from the heat and do a set test (page 10). If the marmalade isn't thick enough, return the pan to the heat for a few minutes, and then repeat the test.

Wash the jars, lids, and bands in very hot soapy water, rinse them well, and place them upside down on a clean towel to drain.

Spoon the marmalade into the jars, leaving a half inch of headroom to allow for expansion during freezing. Wipe the rims with a clean wet cloth or paper towel, add the lids and bands, and finger tighten the bands.

Label the jars. Cool completely and tighten the bands before storing the jars in the refrigerator or freezer.

QUICK IDEAS // A nice balance of tangy and sweet, this marmalade is delicious on thickly sliced pumpernickel with very sharp cheddar cheese. Serve it alongside chicken or lamb curry. Spoon it over a ricotta tart and sprinkle on chopped fresh parsley or basil for an elegant first course or a light meal.

hot and sweet carrot relish

MAKES ABOUT 3 HALF-PINTS

This sweet relish gets a little heat from the jalapeño. If you want the relish hotter, leave in the seeds and membranes; for a milder relish, substitute a sweet pepper.

Sweet winter storage carrots are perfect for this relish. Peel winter carrots before shredding them because their skins can be a bit tough. There's no need to peel fresh summer carrots.

1 pound carrots, coarsely shredded (about 4 cups)	2 teaspoons yellow mustard seeds
3 tablespoons minced jalapeño pepper	½ teaspoon salt
3 tablespoons minced garlic	⅔ cup cider vinegar
1 tablespoon finely grated fresh ginger	½ cup unsweetened apple juice
1 tablespoon coriander seeds, toasted and crushed	¼ cup lime juice
	½ cup packed light brown sugar

Combine all of the ingredients in a 10-inch sauté pan set over medium heat, and bring it to a boil. Lower the heat and simmer, stirring occasionally, until the liquid is reduced and the mixture is sticky and glossy, about 20 minutes. If the relish appears too dry, add a little apple juice or water.

Wash the jars, lids, and bands in very hot soapy water, rinse them well, and place them upside down on a clean towel to drain.

Spoon the relish into the jars, leaving a half inch of headroom to allow for expansion during freezing. Cover each jar with a square of wax paper slightly larger than the jar opening, fold in the corners with a clean spoon, and gently push down so some of the syrup comes up over the wax paper. Wipe the rims with a clean wet cloth or paper towel, add the lids and bands, and finger tighten the bands.

Label the jars. Allow the relish to cool completely and tighten the bands before storing in the refrigerator or freezer.

QUICK IDEAS // Serve this relish warm as a side dish to grilled or roast chicken, room temperature with cured meats, and cold on a picnic with ham, cheese, and a baguette. It's delicious stuffed into a pita with salty feta. Try it in quesadillas filled with White Bean Dip (page 21).

corn

What to do with the glorious bounty of sweet corn? It's the one vegetable we long for until it comes into season; when it arrives, we devour ears and ears of it three times a day. Then, although it's hard to believe, come early September, we are weary of all that corn. Here's what to do!

corn salsa

MAKES 5 TO 6 HALF-PINTS

Paste (or Roma) tomatoes work especially well in this salsa because they have fewer seeds, but feel free to use a combination of tomato varieties. We don't bother removing the skins. Vary the heat in this salsa by choosing different kinds of peppers. It's important to use fresh corn for the best taste.

VEGETABLES

2 cups corn kernels
1½ cups seeded and medium-diced
     paste (or Roma) tomatoes
1 cup medium-diced sweet pepper
½ cup medium-diced poblano pepper
½ cup medium-diced sweet yellow onion
½ cup medium-diced red onion
1 tablespoon minced garlic

BRINE

1 cup cider vinegar
1 tablespoon sugar
2 teaspoons salt
1 teaspoon ground cumin
1 teaspoon ground coriander

Combine the vinegar, sugar, salt, cumin, and coriander in a 10-inch sauté pan, and stir to mix well. Add the corn, tomatoes, sweet and hot peppers, yellow and red onion, and garlic, and bring to a gentle boil over medium heat. Lower the heat a little, and simmer for about 5 to 10 minutes. You want the vegetables to be fairly firm and crunchy. Stir occasionally to prevent sticking.

Wash the jars, lids, and bands in very hot soapy water, rinse them well, and place them upside down on a clean towel to drain.

Spoon the salsa into the jars. Remember to leave a half inch of headroom to allow for expansion during freezing. Wipe the rims with a clean wet cloth or paper towel, add the lids and bands, and finger tighten the bands.

Label the jars. Cool completely and tighten the bands before storing the jars in the refrigerator or freezer.

QUICK IDEAS // For a just-made taste, add fresh cilantro to this salsa just before serving it. The salsa is great with chips, on tortillas or nachos, as a garnish to black bean soup, and spooned onto grilled steak, pork, or chicken.

hot and sweet pickled corn

MAKES 6 HALF-PINTS

Adjust the heat level in this classic pickle by choosing the right peppers—Fresnos tend to be sweet; habaneros pack big heat; jalapeños fall somewhere in between.

VEGETABLES
4½ cups corn kernels
1 cup finely diced onion
3 tablespoons minced garlic
3 Fresno peppers, halved lengthwise
but not seeded

BRINE
1½ cups cider vinegar
¾ cup water
½ cup sugar
1 tablespoon salt
2 tablespoons brown mustard seeds
1 tablespoon crushed red pepper flakes
1 tablespoon fennel seeds

Wash the jars, lids, and bands in very hot soapy water, rinse them well, and place them upside down on a clean towel to drain.

In a medium bowl, mix together the corn, onion, and garlic, and set it aside. Put a half pepper into each jar, and then divide the corn mixture among the jars.

Combine the vinegar, water, sugar, salt, mustard seeds, crushed red pepper flakes, and fennel seeds in a medium saucepan, set it over medium-high heat, and bring it to a boil. Stir to dissolve the sugar and salt. Pour the brine over the vegetables, and spoon the spices into the jars. Remember to leave a half inch of headroom. Using a spoon handle, work the spices into the corn.

Cover each jar with a square of wax paper slightly larger than the jar opening, fold in the corners with a clean spoon, and gently push down so some of the brine comes up over the wax paper. Wipe the rims with a clean wet cloth or paper towel, add the lids and bands, and finger tighten the bands.

Label the jars. Cool completely and tighten the bands before storing the jars in the refrigerator or freezer. Let the pickled corn rest for a few weeks before eating to allow the flavors to marry.

QUICK IDEAS // Great at a barbecue! Toss this corn with black beans for a salad. Serve it over tacos and burritos. Add chopped tomatoes to make a salsa for chips.

sweet spicy corn and cabbage relish

MAKES ABOUT 5 HALF-PINTS

Super quick and ultra easy to make, this relish captures the sense of summer in a couple of jars.

BRINE
- 1 cup cider vinegar
- ¼ cup water
- ¼ cup sugar
- 1½ teaspoons English mustard powder
- 1½ teaspoons yellow mustard seeds
- 1½ teaspoons celery seeds
- 1 teaspoon salt

VEGETABLES
- 2½ cups corn kernels
- 1½ cups medium-diced red cabbage
- ½ cup medium-diced onion
- ½ cup medium-diced poblano pepper
- ½ cup medium-diced sweet pepper
- 2 teaspoons minced garlic

In a 10-inch sauté pan, stir together the vinegar, water, sugar, mustard powder, mustard seeds, celery seeds, and salt. Add the corn, cabbage, onion, hot and sweet peppers, and garlic. Set the pan over medium heat, and bring to a gentle boil. Lower the heat and simmer, stirring occasionally, until the vegetables are tender-crisp, about 10 to 15 minutes.

Wash the jars, lids, and bands in very hot soapy water, rinse them well, and place them upside down on a clean towel to drain.

Spoon the relish into the jars, remembering to leave a half inch of headroom to allow for expansion during freezing. Wipe the rims with a clean wet cloth or paper towel, add the lids and bands, and finger tighten the bands. Label the jars. Cool completely and tighten the bands before storing the jars in the refrigerator or freezer.

QUICK IDEAS // Serve this relish with tacos, chili, and black bean soup. Stir it into salsa, and serve it with chips. Toss the relish with red beans for a picnic salad.

cucumbers

We use the standard slicing and the English cucumbers in these recipes because they're available year round. Super-skinny, long English cukes have fewer seeds and less moisture than standard cucumbers.

savory cucumber relish

MAKES ABOUT 2 HALF-PINTS

Most traditional cucumber relishes are overly sweet and mask the cucumber's bright, refreshing flavors. This savory version is terrific in a tartar sauce, piled onto hot dogs, and served with cold meats.

1 to 1⅓ pounds cucumbers	¼ cup sugar
1 cup coarsely chopped onions	1 tablespoon minced garlic
2 tablespoons salt	2 teaspoons dill seeds
4¼ cups cold water	2 teaspoons yellow mustard seeds
1 cup cider vinegar	½ teaspoon ground turmeric

Peel the cucumbers, cut them in half lengthwise, scoop out the seeds, and cut them into large chunks. Put the cucumbers and the onions into a food processor fitted with a steel blade. Pulse the vegetables to finely chop them, being careful not to overprocess.

In a large bowl, whisk together the salt and 4 cups of water until the salt is dissolved. Add the chopped vegetables, and mix well. Cover the bowl and set it aside, out of direct sunlight, for 2 hours.

Turn the vegetables into a colander, and rinse them well under running cold water to remove the salt. Drain well, pressing out the excess water with a spoon.

Put the vinegar, sugar, ¼ cup of water, garlic, dill seeds, mustard seeds, and turmeric into a 10-inch sauté pan set over medium-high heat. Bring the mixture to a boil; then lower it to a simmer. Stir in the vegetables, and simmer, stirring occasionally, until most of the liquid has evaporated from the pan, about 10 minutes. The relish is done when you can drag a large spoon across the bottom of the pan and the mixture holds its shape.

Wash the jars, lids, and bands in very hot soapy water, rinse them well, and place them upside down on a clean towel to drain.

Spoon the relish into the jars, leaving a half inch of headroom to allow for expansion during freezing. Wipe the rims with a clean wet cloth or paper towel, add the lids and bands, and finger tighten the bands.

Label the jars. Cool completely and tighten the bands before storing the jars in the refrigerator or freezer.

QUICK IDEAS // Add a spoonful or two of relish to a potato salad or a chicken salad. Whisk with mayonnaise into a thousand island dressing. It's great on grilled fish and, of course, hot dogs!

sweet pickled cucumber slices

MAKES ABOUT 4 HALF-PINTS

Slender, seedless English cucumbers are thin-skinned and perfect in this pickle. It's also good made with the smaller Persian or Lebanese cucumbers, available in Middle Eastern markets.

1¼	pounds cucumbers, thinly sliced	½	cup sugar
1½	cups thinly sliced onion (about ¼ pound)	1	tablespoon yellow mustard seeds
¼	cup salt	1	teaspoon caraway seeds
1½	cups cider vinegar	½	teaspoon ground turmeric

Combine the sliced cucumbers and onions with the salt in a large stainless steel or glass bowl. Toss to coat well, cover, and place in refrigerator for at least 12 hours. With a clean spoon, turn the cucumbers a few times in the salt brine.

Place the cucumbers and onions in a colander, and rinse them well under cold running water. Turn them into a bowl of cold water to soak for a few minutes. Drain well.

Wash the jars, lids, and bands in very hot soapy water, rinse them well, and place them upside down on a clean towel to drain.

Combine the vinegar, sugar, mustard seeds, caraway seeds, and turmeric in a 10-inch sauté pan, and bring to a boil over high heat. Add the well-drained cucumbers and onions to the pan, and return to a boil. Boil for exactly 2 minutes, and turn off heat.

Place a sieve over a deep bowl, pour in the cooked cucumbers and onions, and drain well. Fill the jars with the cucumber slices, pressing down so they fit and leaving a half inch of headroom.

Return the brine to the sauté pan. Measure the depth of the brine using the dipstick method (page 9). Bring the brine back to a boil over high heat, and cook until it has reduced by half, about 10 minutes.

Pour the brine into the jars. Cover each jar with a square of wax paper slightly larger than the jar opening, fold in the corners with a clean spoon, and gently push down so some of the brine comes up over the wax paper. Wipe the rims with a clean wet cloth or paper towel, add the lids and bands, and finger tighten the bands.

Label the jars. Cool completely and tighten the lids before storing the jars in the refrigerator. Let the pickles rest for at least 2 weeks before eating to allow the flavors to blend.

QUICK IDEAS // Top crostini spread with cream cheese or tangy chèvre with these pickled cukes. Arrange the slices over grilled or poached salmon. Pile them onto lamb burgers. You may have some extra brine to whisk into a salad dressing or tartar sauce.

eggplant

Eggplant is the surprise element in these preserves. Its delicate flavor takes beautifully to stronger ingredients, especially the Middle Eastern seasonings.

eggplant chutney with cardamom and pomegranate molasses

MAKES ABOUT 3 HALF-PINTS

Pomegranate molasses, available in Middle Eastern markets, is thick, sweet, and tangy and adds a depth of flavor to the mix. The Fresno pepper gives this just the right amount of heat.

3 tablespoons olive oil

1 pound eggplant, unpeeled, coarsely chopped

½ pound tomatoes, coarsely chopped

½ cup sugar

¼ cup lemon juice

¼ cup balsamic vinegar

¼ cup minced poblano pepper, not seeded

2 tablespoons minced Fresno pepper, not seeded

2 tablespoons pomegranate molasses

2 teaspoons ground ginger

1 teaspoon ground cinnamon

1 teaspoon salt

½ teaspoon cardamom seeds, crushed

Heat the oil in a 10-inch sauté pan, add the eggplant, and cook until the eggplant is soft and starts to take on color. Add the remaining ingredients, lower the heat a little, and simmer the chutney, stirring occasionally, until it becomes thick and jammy, about 10 minutes. The chutney is done when you can drag a spoon across the bottom and the mixture holds its shape.

Wash the jars, lids, and bands in very hot soapy water, rinse them well, and place them upside down on a clean towel to drain.

Spoon the chutney into the jars, leaving a half inch of headroom to allow for expansion during freezing. Wipe the rims with a clean wet cloth or paper towel, add the lids and bands, and finger tighten the bands.

Label the jars. Cool completely and tighten the bands before storing the jars in the refrigerator or freezer.

NOTE: If you can't find cardamom seeds, use cardamom pods and crack them open to release the seeds. To open the pods and release the seeds, place them in a resealable plastic bag and smash them with a heavy rolling pin. To crush the seeds, either use a mortar and pestle or put the seeds back in the plastic bag and crush them with the rolling pin.

QUICK IDEAS // Stuff this chutney into a pita sandwich with crumbled feta. Serve it on top of bruschetta spread with chèvre. Set it out as a dip for pita chips. It's lovely with roasted leg of lamb or lamb skewers or stirred into yogurt to top off a curry.

eggplant dip with poblano peppers

MAKES ABOUT 4 HALF-PINTS

Don't let the long roasting time deter you from making this creamy, spicy dip. When winter comes around, you will be happy to have this dip on hand and wishing you had made more; it freezes beautifully. Any variety of eggplant will work well.

3	to 3½ pounds eggplant	1	tablespoon cider vinegar
3	poblano peppers	¼	cup olive oil
½	cup oven-dried tomatoes (page 79)	1	tablespoon ground cumin
	or ¼ cup sun-dried tomatoes	1	tablespoon chopped fresh oregano
3	tablespoons lemon juice	1	teaspoon salt
1½	tablespoons minced garlic	10	to 15 grinds black pepper

Preheat the oven to 400 degrees. Pierce the eggplants on all sides with a fork. Place the eggplants and the peppers on a parchment-lined baking sheet.

Roast the peppers until they are blistered on all sides, about 30 minutes. Place the roasted peppers in a bowl, and cover it with plastic wrap to steam and loosen the skins. Peel the peppers, and remove the seeds. Dice the peppers, and set them aside.

Roast the eggplants on the middle rack in the oven, turning them every 30 minutes, until very soft, very wrinkled, and collapsed, about 1 to 2 hours, depending on size. When the eggplants have cooled, slice them in half lengthwise, and scoop out the flesh and juices. You should have about 3 cups.

Turn the eggplant pulp, peppers, dried tomatoes, lemon juice, minced garlic, and vinegar into a food processor fitted with a steel blade, and pulse a few times. Add the olive oil, cumin, oregano, salt, and pepper, and pulse to create a chunky puree. Taste, and adjust the seasoning.

Wash the jars, lids, and bands in very hot soapy water, rinse them well, and place them upside down on a clean towel to drain.

Spoon the dip into the jars, leaving a half inch of headroom to allow for expansion during freezing. Wipe the rims with a clean wet cloth or paper towel, add the lids and bands, and finger tighten the bands.

Label the jars. Cool completely before tightening the bands and storing the jars in the refrigerator or freezer.

QUICK IDEAS // Delicious served as a dip, this is also good as a sandwich filling and a pizza topping. Warm the dip to serve over grilled chicken or lamb.

fennel

Fennel is as crunchy as celery with mild hints of licorice. It's great pickled: it retains its texture in the brine and takes nicely to the sharper flavors.

fennel and onion confit

MAKES 3 TO 4 HALF-PINTS

The term *confit* comes from the French word *confire,* meaning "to preserve," and applies to any food that's slowly cooked in a fat. In this recipe, the fennel is simmered in olive oil to become meltingly tender and very flavorful.

When you clean the fennel, cut off the top leaves but keep the small fronds that may be inside; they will add a delicious fennel flavor to the confit.

1 pound fennel, finely diced (4 cups)	¼ cup white balsamic vinegar
3½ cups finely diced onion	2 tablespoons minced garlic
¼ cup olive oil	2 tablespoons minced fresh rosemary
1½ teaspoons salt	10 to 15 grinds black pepper

Combine the fennel, onion, olive oil, and salt in a 10-inch sauté pan set over medium-low heat. When it begins to sizzle, cover the pan and simmer for about 45 minutes, stirring occasionally, until very soft.

Remove the lid, stir in the vinegar, garlic, rosemary, and pepper, and simmer until most of the liquid has evaporated and the confit looks glossy and soft, about 15 minutes. Taste, and adjust the seasoning.

Wash the jars, lids, and bands in very hot soapy water, rinse them well, and place them upside down on a clean towel to drain.

Spoon the confit into the jars, leaving a half inch of headroom to allow for expansion during freezing. Wipe the rims with a clean wet cloth or paper towel, add the lids and bands, and finger tighten the bands.

Label the jars. Cool completely and tighten the bands before storing the jars in the refrigerator or freezer.

QUICK IDEAS // Spread the confit over roast pork before it comes out of the oven or on a pork chop before pulling it from the grill. Toss it with pasta and some sharp cheese. It's great on a warm hoagie or meatball sandwich and pizza.

pickled fennel with lemongrass

MAKES 2 PINTS

The key to this pickle is mild, fragrant lemongrass. If lemongrass isn't available, substitute about 4 wide bands of lemon zest.

1 pound fennel, thinly sliced (about 5 cups)	2 teaspoons fennel seeds
4 to 6 small fennel fronds	1 cup rice vinegar
3 (3-inch) pieces lemongrass, slightly bruised and halved lengthwise	¼ cup water
	2 tablespoons sugar
2 bay leaves	½ teaspoon salt
2 tablespoons pink peppercorns	

Bring a large pot of water to a boil over high heat. Ready a bowl of ice water. Blanch the fennel slices in the boiling water, about 30 seconds. Drain. Immediately place the fennel in the bowl of ice water to stop the cooking. Drain and set aside the fennel. ·

Wash the jars, lids, and bands in very hot soapy water, rinse them well, and place them upside down on a clean towel to drain.

Fill the jars with the fennel slices. Place the fennel fronds on top of the fennel slices or tuck them in between the slices as you fill the jars. Add the lemongrass and bay leaves to each jar; then add the pink peppercorns and fennel seeds.

Put the vinegar, water, sugar, and salt in a small saucepan set over low heat, and stir until the sugar and salt have dissolved. Pour the brine into the jars, leaving about a half inch of headroom.

Cover each jar with a square of wax paper slightly larger than the jar opening, fold in the corners with a clean spoon, and gently push down so some of the brine comes up over the wax paper. Wipe the rims with a clean wet cloth or paper towel, add the lids and bands, and finger tighten the bands.

Label the jars. Let the jars rest in the refrigerator for a couple of weeks to allow the flavors to marry. The fennel will keep nicely for several months.

QUICK IDEAS // This fennel is perfect with fish cooked any way—fried, grilled, sautéed, baked, or broiled.

garlic

We use garlic in all its different iterations–scapes, young fresh bulbs, mature cloves. Thanks to the farmers at our markets, you can find deliciously fresh, plump bulbs of garlic throughout the season.

garlic scape pesto with lemon thyme

MAKES ABOUT 4 QUARTER-PINTS

Garlic scapes are the flower buds of garlic plants. Growers cut them off in late June so the bulbs will develop. The scapes are just a little milder than garlic bulbs, but plenty assertive.

This northern version of a classic Italian sauce calls for local nuts, cheese, and oil. If you don't grow your own scapes, or know someone who does, find them in farmers markets and co-ops.

10 large garlic scapes (about ¼ pound)	1 tablespoon chopped fresh lemon thyme
⅓ cup toasted, coarsely chopped hazelnuts	½ teaspoon salt
⅓ cup packed coarsely shredded aged hard cheese, such as Wisconsin Sartori SarVecchio	10 to 15 grinds black pepper
	⅓ cup sunflower oil, plus more for topping the jars

Coarsely chop the garlic scapes; you should have about 1 heaping cup. In a food processor fitted with a steel blade, process the garlic scapes, hazelnuts, cheese, lemon thyme, salt, and pepper into a fine, dry texture. Scrape the sides to make sure it's all chopped. With the food processor running, add the oil in a slow, steady stream to create a smooth paste. If the pesto appears a little dry, add a little more oil.

Wash the jars, lids, and bands in very hot soapy water, rinse them well, and place them upside down on a clean towel to drain.

Spoon the pesto into the jars, leaving a half inch of headroom. Smooth out the tops with a clean spoon, and add a thin layer of sunflower oil to the top. The oil helps keep out oxygen that might spoil or discolor the pesto, so it will last longer in the refrigerator. Wipe the rims with a clean wet cloth or paper towel, add the lids and bands, and tighten the bands.

Label the jars. Store the jars in the refrigerator or freezer.

QUICK IDEAS // Toss the pesto with pasta or stir it into rice. Whisk it into mayonnaise to top grilled chicken and steak. Slather the pesto on pizzas and open-faced grilled cheese sandwiches.

indian-spiced garlic chutney

MAKES ABOUT 5 QUARTER-PINTS

The time to make this chutney is in late summer and early fall when local garlic is tender and juicy. The younger and fresher the garlic, the better the chutney will taste.

½ cup white wine vinegar

1 cup sugar

2 tablespoons lemon juice

⅓ cup sunflower oil

1 tablespoon black mustard seeds (see note)

1 tablespoon cumin seeds

1 teaspoon cayenne pepper

2 teaspoons ground fenugreek

½ teaspoon ground turmeric

1 teaspoon salt

½ pound garlic cloves, peeled and finely chopped (about 1¼ cups)

Combine the vinegar and sugar in a 10-inch sauté pan set over medium heat. Bring to a gentle boil, and stir to dissolve the sugar. Lower the heat, and add the lemon juice, oil, mustard seeds, cumin seeds, cayenne, fenugreek, turmeric, salt, and garlic.

Simmer, stirring occasionally, until most of the liquid has evaporated, about 15 minutes. The chutney is done when you can drag a spoon across the bottom of the pan and the mixture holds its shape.

Wash the jars, lids, and bands in very hot soapy water, rinse them well, and place them upside down on a clean towel to drain.

Spoon the chutney into the jars. Remember to leave a half inch of headroom to allow for expansion during freezing. Wipe the rims with a clean wet cloth or paper towel, add the lids and bands, and finger tighten the bands.

Label the jars. Cool completely and tighten the bands before storing the jars in the refrigerator or freezer. Let the chutney mature for at least 1 week before using so the flavors marry.

NOTE: Black mustard seeds are slightly hotter than brown mustard seeds. They are available at Indian markets. If you can't find the black seeds, use the brown and maybe increase the amount a little.

QUICK IDEAS // This sweet and tangy condiment is thick and rich. It's delicious spread over grilled lamb, served alongside curry, and on top of a creamy Camembert cheese.

saffron pickled garlic

The best time to pickle garlic is late July to early August when our farmers markets are full of the sweetest, juiciest bulbs. Pickling mellows the flavor of garlic but retains its crunch.

If the garlic is very fresh, feel free to skip the blanching step. The quick dunk in boiling water just helps loosen the papery skin that sticks to the garlic cloves.

If pink peppercorns are not available, substitute black peppercorns and increase the amount by ¼ teaspoon.

1 pound very fresh and heavy garlic bulbs	1 teaspoon pink peppercorns
5 bay leaves	1 cup cider vinegar
2 teaspoons fennel seeds	¼ cup sugar
1 teaspoon black peppercorns	generous pinch of saffron threads

Fill a medium pot three-quarters full of water, and bring it to a boil. Blanch the garlic bulbs for about 30 to 60 seconds. Turn the bulbs into a colander, and rinse them well under cold water. This step helps loosen the skins, but doesn't cook the garlic.

Pat the garlic dry in a clean kitchen towel, break open the bulbs, and peel the cloves by slipping off the skins with your finger or a paring knife.

Wash the jars, lids, and bands in very hot soapy water, rinse them well, and place them upside down on a clean towel to drain.

Add 1 bay leaf to each jar and divide the garlic cloves among the jars. Divide the fennel seeds and peppercorns among the jars.

Combine the vinegar, sugar, and saffron threads in a small saucepan set over medium heat, and bring to a gentle boil for several minutes. Pour the hot brine over the garlic, leaving about a half inch of headroom in the jars.

Wipe the rims with a clean wet cloth or paper towel, add the lids and bands, and finger tighten the bands.

Label the jars. Cool completely before tightening the bands and storing the jars in the refrigerator.

QUICK IDEAS // Toss these cloves of garlic into the pan when roasting chicken or pork. Use them to make pesto or beat them into unsalted butter. Slice them into slivers to scatter over pizza and flatbread.

mushrooms

Mushrooms are big in Nordic cuisine: intrepid foragers head into the damp, cool woods to seek out morels, chanterelles, trumpets, and hen of the woods. Preserving mushrooms with spices and oil emphasizes their meatiness. These recipes make delicious use of a big haul of wild mushrooms as well as cultivated shiitake, oyster, portobello, and cremini mushrooms.

preserved mushrooms

MAKES ABOUT 3 HALF-PINTS

Inspired by the Nordic method of preserving foods in both vinegar and oil, these mushrooms are earthy, densely textured, and elegant.

If you are a lucky forager, or know one, make these with small, firm chanterelles or trumpets. But cultivated cremini work wonderfully too.

SPICE BAG

- 2 large sprigs thyme
- 1 tablespoon coarsely chopped garlic
- 2 dried árbol or other hot chili peppers (see note on page 56)
- 2 wide bands lemon zest
- 1 teaspoon black peppercorns
- 2 bay leaves

- 1 pound wild mushrooms or small cremini mushrooms

BRINE

- 2 cups rice vinegar
- 1 cup water
- 2 teaspoons salt

about 1½ cups sunflower or other neutral oil (see note on page 56)

Put the thyme, garlic, chili peppers, lemon zest, peppercorns, and bay leaves in a spice bag (or make one out of cheesecloth and close it with kitchen string or a toothpick).

With a damp paper towel or cloth, wipe the dirt from the mushrooms. Trim the ends, and place the mushrooms in a large bowl.

Combine the vinegar, water, salt, and spice bag in a medium saucepan. Bring the liquid to a gentle boil over medium heat, and stir to dissolve the salt. Remove the pan from the heat, and cool for 5 minutes. Pour the cooled liquid over the mushrooms, and transfer the spice bag to the bowl. To keep the mushrooms submerged, cover the mushrooms with parchment or wax paper, and weight it with a plate topped with a clean, heavy object, such as a brick in a resealable bag, a pot, or a bowl. (A little of the brine

continued on page 56

from the mushrooms should come up over the plate.) Marinate the mushrooms at room temperature for at least 12 hours.

Remove and discard the spice bag. Drain the mushrooms well, reserving the pickling brine for other uses (see note below).

Wash the jars, lids, and bands in very hot soapy water, rinse them well, and place them upside down on a clean towel to drain.

Divide the mushrooms among the jars. Fill the jars with the sunflower oil to just barely cover the mushrooms. Cover each jar with a square of wax paper slightly larger than the jar opening, fold in the corners with a clean spoon, and push down lightly on the wax paper. Allow some of the oil to come up over the paper to ensure the mushrooms stay submerged in the oil. Add more oil if needed. Wipe the rims with a clean wet cloth or paper towel, add the lids and bands, and tighten the bands.

Label the jars. Store the jars in the refrigerator. Let the mushrooms marinate for a few days before using.

NOTE: Pretty, red árbol peppers, aka bird's beak and rat's tail peppers, are bold and smoky, so use them with care. You can opt to use a milder dried chili for less heat.

NOTE: You can use olive oil instead, but it hardens in the refrigerator. You'll need to bring the mushrooms to room temperature before using them.

NOTE: To reserve the brine for other uses, strain it through a cloth-lined sieve and pour it into a saucepan. Heat the strained brine for a few minutes. Pour the brine into a clean glass jar, and store it in the refrigerator. It will keep for weeks. You can use this brine to make quick pickles of onions or thin-sliced carrots and fennel. The brine's lovely earthy notes work well in salad dressings.

QUICK IDEAS // Serve the mushrooms straight from the jar on an antipasto plate. Mix them with sour cream or yogurt to garnish roast beef or pork. They're delicious piled high on dense rye or pumpernickel bread.

mushroom ketchup

Long before the tomato was the king of ketchup, mushrooms were simmered into spicy, smooth condiments. Primarily used to sauce roast beef, lamb, and pork, mushroom ketchup was also stirred into soups and stews to add flavor and body. The flavor and texture of this condiment will depend on the variety of mushrooms you choose—fresh foraged, cultivated, or a mix of fresh and dried—play around, have fun!

1½ pounds cremini or other mushrooms, cleaned and sliced	½ cup sugar
2 tablespoons salt	2 teaspoons ground allspice
1 ounce dried porcini mushrooms	½ teaspoon ground ginger
2 cups boiling water	¼ teaspoon ground cloves
¼ cup coarsely chopped shallots	¼ teaspoon ground cinnamon
1 tablespoon coarsely chopped garlic	½ teaspoon ground mace
1 cup cider vinegar	1 tablespoon smoked sweet paprika

In a large bowl, layer the fresh mushrooms with the salt. Cover the bowl, and let the mushrooms macerate at room temperature for 8 hours or overnight.

Put the porcini mushrooms in a small bowl, add 2 cups of boiling water, and soak for 30 minutes. Drain well, reserving 1 cup of the soaking liquid.

Turn the salted mushrooms into a colander, and rinse them under running cold water to remove the salt. Drain well.

Working in batches, use a food processor fitted with a steel blade to puree the fresh and dried mushrooms, shallots, and garlic into a rich, thick paste. Put the mixture into a 10-inch sauté pan.

Stir the vinegar, reserved soaking liquid from the porcini, and sugar into the pan, and add the allspice, ginger, cloves, cinnamon, mace, and paprika. Bring the mixture to a gentle boil over medium heat. Reduce to a simmer, and stir occasionally. As it cooks down, the mash will release bursts of hot steam, so stir cautiously.

Simmer the mushroom mash until most of the liquid has evaporated and the ketchup is thick, about 30 minutes. Add a little water if the mash looks too dry. Taste, and adjust the seasonings. Remove from heat.

Set a medium mesh sieve over a deep bowl. Working in batches, press the mushroom mash through the sieve, scraping the underside of the sieve with a clean spoon. Discard the remaining mushroom pulp.

Wash the jars, lids, and bands in very hot soapy water, rinse them well, and place them upside down on a clean towel to drain.

continued on next page

Spoon the ketchup into the jars, leaving a half inch of headroom to allow for expansion during freezing. Wipe the rims with a clean wet cloth or paper towel, add the lids and bands, and finger tighten the bands.

Label the jars. Cool completely and tighten the bands before storing the jars in the refrigerator or freezer. The ketchup will taste better if allowed to mature for a couple of weeks before eating.

· NOTE: To clean mushrooms, use a damp piece of paper towel or cloth to carefully remove any dirt. Cut off the dried ends. If using foraged mushrooms, dip them in salted water to remove dirt and any bugs.

QUICK IDEAS // Spoon mushroom ketchup onto grilled rib eye and burgers. Stir it into soups, stews, casseroles, and potpie filling.

onions

Pickled onions have an uncanny, magical ability to transform sandwiches, burgers, and tacos. We can find great onions year round for these easy, satisfying recipes.

crispy pickled red onions

MAKES 4 HALF-PINTS

Don't be alarmed as you make this pickle: the red onions will become slightly grayish purple as they rest in the salt. But when they hit the vinegar, they will return to their lively magenta hue.

1 pound red onions, cut in half and sliced thin (about 4 cups)	2 teaspoons whole allspice
½ cup salt	2 teaspoons black peppercorns
2 teaspoons coriander seeds	4 small dried árbol peppers (see note)
2 teaspoons yellow mustard seeds	1½ cups cider vinegar
	3 tablespoons sugar

In a medium bowl, work the onions and salt together with your hands. Cover the bowl, and let the onions macerate at room temperature for at least 6 hours or overnight.

Rinse the onions well under cold running water to remove all the salt. Place the onions in a bowl of ice water for about 30 minutes. Drain well.

Wash the jars, lids, and bands in very hot soapy water, rinse them well, and place them upside down on a clean towel to drain.

Divide the onions among the jars. In each jar, place ½ teaspoon coriander seeds, ½ teaspoon yellow mustard seeds, ½ teaspoon whole allspice, ½ teaspoon black peppercorns, and 1 dried árbol pepper.

In a small saucepan, whisk together the vinegar and sugar. Set the pan over medium heat, and stir until the sugar dissolves.

Pour the brine into the jars, leaving a half inch of headroom. Cover each jar with a square of wax paper slightly larger than the jar opening, fold in the corners with a clean spoon, and gently push down so some of the brine comes up over the wax paper. Wipe the rims with a clean wet cloth or paper towel, add the lids and bands, and tighten the bands.

Label the jars. Store the onions in the refrigerator for at least 1 week before eating them to allow the flavors to marry. The longer you wait, the better they will taste.

NOTE: Pretty, red árbol peppers, aka bird's beak and rat's tail peppers, are bold and smoky, so use them with care. You can opt to use a milder dried chili for less heat.

QUICK IDEAS // These red onions are perfect on tacos, in grilled cheese sandwiches, tossed into a green salad, and stirred into the filling for deviled eggs.

onion pomegranate marmalade

MAKES ABOUT 4 HALF-PINTS

Despite the name "marmalade," with its implied sweetness, this classic British condiment is served with a variety of roasted meats and savory pies. Soaking the onions in water first mellows their sharpness (unless you're using sweet onions, such as Vidalias). Find pomegranate molasses in Middle Eastern markets and the ethnic section of some grocery stores.

2 pounds onions, cut in to thin slices (about 8 cups)	½ cup cider vinegar
3 tablespoons olive oil	2 tablespoons pomegranate molasses
½ teaspoon salt	1 tablespoon finely grated fresh ginger
½ cup packed light brown sugar	2 teaspoon crushed red pepper flakes

Place the sliced onions in a large bowl, and cover them with cold water and a few ice cubes. Let the onions sit for about 15 minutes; then drain and pat the onions dry between two large kitchen towels.

Heat the olive oil in a 10-inch sauté pan; then add the onion slices and salt. Cook, uncovered, over low heat until the onions are very soft and have collapsed to about half the volume, about 15 minutes.

Stir in the brown sugar. When it's dissolved, add the vinegar, pomegranate molasses, ginger, and crushed red pepper flakes. Simmer over medium-low heat, stirring occasionally, until most of the liquid has evaporated, about 30 minutes. Taste, and adjust the seasoning.

Wash the jars, lids, and bands in very hot soapy water, rinse them well, and place them upside down on a clean towel to drain.

Spoon the marmalade into the jars, leaving a half inch of headroom to allow for expansion during freezing. Wipe the rims with a clean wet cloth or paper towel, add the lids and bands, and finger tighten the bands.

Label the jars. Cool completely before tightening the bands and storing the jars in the refrigerator or freezer.

QUICK IDEAS // This sweet, tangy condiment is great on sausages, pork, and chicken; alongside potpies; and smashed into mashed potatoes. Spoon the marmalade on crostini or bruschetta spread with chèvre, feta, or a creamy blue cheese.

parsnips

This pale member of the carrot family makes a beautiful condiment. Its sweet and distinctly earthy flavors are a quiet backdrop for the world's spices. Try including parsnips in our carrot recipes.

parsnip and grapefruit relish

MAKES ABOUT 3 HALF-PINTS

Toasting spices draws out their oils and amps up their flavors. To toast the coriander seeds, set a dry cast-iron skillet over medium heat and add the seeds. Shake the pan a few times; they'll be ready in a couple of minutes. You want them to smell toasted but not burned.

1 pound parsnips, coarsely shredded (about 4 cups)

3 tablespoons minced jalapeño pepper

3 tablespoons minced garlic

1 tablespoon finely grated fresh ginger

1 tablespoon coriander seeds, toasted and crushed

1 tablespoon finely grated grapefruit zest

1 teaspoon yellow mustard seeds

½ teaspoon salt

⅔ cup cider vinegar

½ cup unsweetened apple juice

¼ cup fresh grapefruit juice

½ cup sugar

Combine all of the ingredients in a 10-inch sauté pan, and bring the mixture to a boil over medium heat. Lower the heat and simmer, uncovered, stirring until the mixture becomes thick, sticky, and glossy, about 15 minutes.

Wash the jars, lids, and bands in very hot soapy water, rinse them well, and place them upside down on a clean towel to drain.

Spoon the relish into the jars, leaving a half inch of headroom to allow for expansion during freezing. Cover each jar with a square of wax paper slightly larger than the jar opening, fold in the corners with a clean spoon, and gently push down so some of the liquid comes up over the wax paper. Wipe the rims with a clean wet cloth or paper towel, add the lids and bands, and finger tighten the bands.

Label the jars. Cool completely before tightening the bands and storing the jars in the refrigerator or freezer.

QUICK IDEAS // Tangy, sweet, and hot, this relish is terrific with beef stew, braised lamb shanks, and German sausages. It works magic on cottage cheese. Try it on quesadillas with the White Bean Dip (page 21) or refried beans.

parsnip lime marmalade
with chili and coriander

Old-time vegetable marmalades and jams evolved in the 1700s, when home kitchens were short on fruit but long on root cellar vegetables. Parsnips, carrots, and beets are all high in natural sugars and work beautifully in savory and sweet condiments. Make this marmalade in the winter, after the parsnips have been frost-kissed, their carbohydrates converted to sugars.

⅓ pound limes	¾ cup sugar
1 pound parsnips, peeled	1½ teaspoons crushed red pepper flakes
2 cups water	1 teaspoon ground coriander

Scrub the limes well under running water. Remove the hard blossom parts and any blemishes on the skin. Cut the fruit in half lengthwise, and then slice them crosswise as thinly as possible, discarding the seeds. Place the lime slices in a 10-inch sauté pan.

Coarsely grate the peeled parsnips; you should have about 3½ cups. Add the parsnips to the limes, add the water, and stir well. Cover the pan, and let the parsnips and limes macerate for at least 8 hours, and up to 24 hours, to soften the lime skins.

Place a small plate in the freezer for the set test. Add the sugar, crushed red pepper flakes, and coriander to the sauté pan, and set it over medium-high heat. Bring the mixture to a gentle boil and cook, stirring occasionally, until most of the liquid has evaporated and the marmalade is thick and sticky, about 40 minutes.

Remove the pan from the heat, and do a set test (page 10). If the marmalade isn't thick enough, return the pan to the heat for a few minutes, and then repeat the test.

Wash the jars, lids, and bands in very hot soapy water, rinse them well, and place them upside down on a clean towel to drain.

Spoon the marmalade into the jars, remembering to leave a half inch of headroom to allow for expansion during freezing. Wipe the rims with a clean wet cloth or paper towel, add the lids and bands, and finger tighten the bands.

Label the jars. Cool completely before tightening the bands and storing the jars in the refrigerator or freezer.

QUICK IDEAS // Good on its own as a salad, this marmalade is great piled on a ham sandwich and served with cheeses and cured meats.

peppers—hot and sweet

Peppers—chili and bell—make bright, fresh-tasting pickles and relishes. They remain colorful and crisp when pickled. The range of heat varies in chilies, so add them cautiously. Their oils can be searing: wear gloves or wash your hands as soon as you're done working with them and do not touch your eyes.

roasted red pepper dip

MAKES ABOUT 4 HALF-PINTS

This zesty dip is a pretty red, and you can vary the color by adding an orange or yellow pepper to the mix. Do not use green peppers, because they're just not sweet. To speed up the roasting and cut down on cleaning, we advise using a foil-lined pan.

2½ pounds sweet red peppers, halved lengthwise, stemmed, and seeded

½ pound hot red peppers, halved lengthwise, stemmed, and seeded

5 large garlic cloves

¼ cup sherry vinegar

¼ cup sugar

½ teaspoon salt

Preheat the oven to 450 degrees. Place the peppers skin side up on a foil-lined baking pan and roast, turning frequently, until the peppers are wrinkled and soft, about 30 to 40 minutes. Turn the peppers into a bowl, and cover it with plastic wrap to steam and loosen the skins.

While the peppers are roasting, put the garlic onto a foil-lined pan and roast, shaking the pan occasionally, until golden, about 10 to 20 minutes. Set the garlic aside.

Peel the peppers while holding them over the bowl of a food processor fitted with a steel blade; you want to capture the peppers' juices. Add the flesh of the peppers and the roasted garlic to the juices in the food processor, and puree until smooth.

Transfer the puree to a 10-inch sauté pan, and stir in the vinegar, sugar, and salt. Over medium heat, bring the mixture to a gentle boil. Lower the heat and simmer, stirring occasionally, until the dip thickens, about 15 minutes. It will continue to thicken as it cools.

Wash the jars, lids, and bands in very hot soapy water, rinse them well, and place them upside down on a clean towel to drain.

Spoon the dip into the jars, leaving a half inch of headroom to allow for expansion during freezing. Wipe the rims with a clean wet cloth or paper towel, add the lids and bands, and finger tighten the bands.

Label the jars. Cool completely and tighten the bands before storing the jars in the refrigerator or freezer.

QUICK IDEAS // This dip makes a lovely sauce for grilled or broiled fish and lamb kabobs. Stir it into hummus or yogurt for a chip or veggie dip. Toss it with roasted new potatoes, pasta, and rice.

sweet hot pepper pickles

A cross between pickled and candied peppers, these slices pack sweet heat. We like a blend of jalapeños and spicy Hinkelhatz peppers, but feel free to try a different mix. The hardest part is letting the pickles rest for up to 4 weeks, but your patience will be rewarded with the bold, bright taste. Be careful handling these peppers—don't touch your eyes! You might choose to wear disposable gloves. This recipe can easily be doubled or even tripled. These pickles last forever in the refrigerator; there's no need to freeze them.

1½ cups sugar	1 teaspoon cumin seeds
1 cup rice vinegar	1 teaspoon yellow mustard seeds
2 tablespoons minced garlic	1 pound mixed hot peppers, thinly sliced
1 teaspoon celery seeds	(about 4 cups)

In a 10-inch sauté pan, combine the sugar, vinegar, garlic, celery seeds, cumin seeds, and mustard seeds. Bring the liquid to a gentle boil, reduce the heat, and simmer for 5 minutes. Add the peppers, and simmer for another 5 minutes.

Wash the jars, lids, and bands in very hot soapy water, rinse them well, and place them upside down on a clean towel to drain.

Using a slotted spoon, transfer the peppers to the jars; then fill the jars with brine. Cover each jar with a square of wax paper slightly larger than the jar opening, fold in the corners with a clean spoon, and gently push down so some of the brine comes up over the wax paper. Wipe the rims with a clean wet cloth or paper towel, add the lids and bands, and finger tighten the bands.

Label the jars. Cool completely before tightening the bands and storing the jars in the refrigerator.

NOTE: You will have extra brine after filling the jars. Use it to make a quick pickle of carrots (cut into sticks or coins) and red onion wedges. Let these pickles rest a few days in the refrigerator before eating.

QUICK IDEAS // You might find yourself eating these pickled peppers straight from the jar, but save a few for nachos and tacos, and for garnishing grilled steak and pork, chilled tomato soup, Bloody Marys, and potato salad.

pepper-packed ketchup

Sweet bell peppers, tart apples, and fragrant spices brew into a lush, complex sauce. In this recipe, there's no need to place the spices in a spice bag; everything gets pureed in a food processor and passed through a sieve.

3	pounds red bell peppers	½	cup packed light brown sugar
1	pound tart apples, coarsely chopped (about 4 cups)	2	teaspoons salt
2	cups coarsely chopped onions	1	tablespoon black peppercorns
2	poblano peppers, stemmed and coarsely chopped, seeds included (about 1 cup)	1	tablespoon yellow mustard seeds
		1	tablespoon black mustard seeds (see note)
2	tablespoons minced garlic	1	tablespoon coriander seeds
1	cup cider vinegar	1	organic lemon, quartered

Preheat the broiler to medium heat. Place the whole bell peppers on a parchment-lined baking pan, and set it on the middle rack. Roast the peppers, rotating often, until they're charred on all sides, about 30 to 40 minutes. Put the peppers into a bowl, and cover it with plastic wrap to steam and loosen the skins. Peel and seed the peppers, and set them aside.

In a food processor fitted with a steel blade, finely chop the apples, onions, poblano peppers, and garlic.

In a 10-inch sauté pan, combine the vinegar, brown sugar, salt, peppercorns, yellow and black mustard seeds, coriander seeds, and lemon. Add the finely chopped vegetables. Set the pan over medium heat, and bring the mixture to a gentle boil. Reduce the heat and simmer, uncovered, stirring occasionally, until the mixture has thickened, about 20 minutes. Add the roasted bell peppers, and continue to simmer, stirring occasionally, until the vegetables are very soft, about 20 minutes. Remove and discard the lemon quarters. Working in batches, puree the mixture in a food processor fitted with a steel blade.

Place a medium mesh sieve over a deep bowl. Working in batches, press the pureed vegetables through the sieve, scraping the underside of the sieve with a clean spoon. Discard the solids left in the sieve.

Wash the jars, lids, and bands in very hot soapy water, rinse them well, and place them upside down on a clean towel to drain.

Spoon the ketchup into the jars. Remember to leave a half inch of headroom to allow for expansion during freezing. Wipe the rims with a clean wet cloth or paper towel, add the lids and bands, and finger tighten the bands.

Label the jars. Cool completely before tightening the lids and storing the jars in the refrigerator or freezer.

NOTE: Black mustard seeds are hotter than brown mustard seeds. They can be found in Indian markets. If they're not available, use brown mustard seeds and add an extra teaspoon.

QUICK IDEAS // Serve pepper ketchup as you would tomato ketchup: on hot dogs and hamburgers and with fries. It's great as a dip for chips and terrific alongside fried chicken or fish.

harissa dip

MAKES 3 TO 4 HALF-PINTS

Garlicky and mildly spicy, this North African condiment relies on ancho chilies (dried poblano peppers) for its warm, smoky heat. It keeps a month or more stored in the refrigerator.

2 teaspoons coriander seeds	2 pounds red bell peppers
2 teaspoons cumin seeds	2 tablespoons minced garlic
2 teaspoons caraway seeds	2 tablespoons cider vinegar
2 ounces dried ancho chilies	1 teaspoon salt
1 cup boiling water	½ cup olive oil

Put the coriander, cumin, and caraway seeds in a dry pan over medium heat. Heat, shaking the pan occasionally, until you can smell their fragrance, about 1 minute. Let the spices cool a bit; then grind them and set them aside.

Preheat the broiler to high, and broil the ancho chilies until they puff up. Rotate the chilies to ensure they don't scorch. Place the broiled chilies in a bowl, and cover them with the boiling water. Soak the chilies for 20 minutes, and then drain them.

On a foil-lined baking sheet, broil the bell peppers, rotating them frequently, until they're blistered but not overly charred, about 30 to 40 minutes. Put the peppers into a bowl, and cover it with plastic wrap to steam and loosen the skins. Peel and seed the peppers while holding them over the bowl of a food processor fitted with a steel blade; you want to capture the peppers' juices. Add the flesh of the peppers to the juices in the food processor.

Remove the stems and seeds from the chilies, and add them to the food processor with the garlic, spices, vinegar, and salt. Pulse the peppers to combine. With the motor running, slowly add the oil, pausing occasionally to scrape down the sides of the bowl.

Wash the jars, lids, and bands in very hot soapy water, rinse them well, and place them upside down on a clean towel to drain.

Spoon the dip into the jars, leaving a half inch of headroom to allow for expansion during freezing. Wipe the rims with a clean wet cloth or paper towel, add the lids and bands, and finger tighten the bands.

Label the jars. Cool completely and tighten the bands before storing the jars in the refrigerator or freezer.

QUICK IDEAS // Harissa's garlicky heat is especially good on sweet vegetables such as squash, carrots, and parsnips. It adds a nice kick to salad dressings and vinaigrettes. Rub it over pork, lamb, and chicken before roasting. A swirl of harissa perks up store-bought hummus.

romesco dip

MAKES ABOUT 5 HALF-PINTS

Romesco is a ruddy, all-purpose home-style sauce from Spain. There's no standard recipe, but it always includes peppers, garlic, olive oil, and nuts, which give it a surprising, pleasing crunch. Use the freshest, sweetest peppers you can find.

3 pounds red bell peppers, quartered, stemmed, and seeded	6 tablespoons olive oil
4 large garlic cloves	¼ cup cider vinegar
¾ pound raw, skin-on almonds (about 2½ cups)	1 teaspoon cayenne pepper
	1 teaspoon salt
	10 to 15 grinds black pepper

Preheat the oven to 400 degrees. Place the peppers skin side up on a foil-lined baking pan, and set the pan on the middle rack. Roast, turning frequently, until the peppers begin to char, about 20 minutes. Put the peppers into a bowl, and cover it with plastic wrap to steam and loosen the skins.

While the peppers are roasting, put the garlic and almonds on a baking pan and roast them, shaking the pan occasionally, until they've begun to turn gold, about 10 minutes. Watch that they don't burn.

Peel the peppers while holding them over the bowl of a food processor fitted with a steel blade; you want to capture the peppers' juices. Put the peppers into the food processor and pulse several times. Add the almonds, garlic, olive oil, vinegar, cayenne, salt, and pepper. Process, pausing to scrape down the sides of the bowl. Be careful not to overprocess; the dip should have a crunch. Taste, and adjust the seasonings.

Wash the jars, lids, and bands in very hot soapy water, rinse them well, and place them upside down on a clean towel to drain.

Spoon the dip into the jars, leaving a half inch of headroom to allow for expansion during freezing. Wipe the rims with a clean wet cloth or paper towel, add the lids and bands, and finger tighten the bands.

Label the jars. Cool completely before tightening the bands and storing the jars in the refrigerator or freezer.

QUICK IDEAS // Inspired by the Spanish sauce with the same name, this dip is terrific tossed with pasta and spooned over rice, grilled chicken, and fish. Serve it as a side dish to cold roast pork.

picante pepper chutney

Combine any sweet and hot peppers in this recipe—thin-walled Italian and California peppers, thick-walled bell peppers, and ripe red jalapeños and poblanos for heat.

2½ pounds mixed sweet red peppers	1 teaspoon ground allspice
½ pound mixed medium-hot red peppers	½ teaspoon salt
2 tablespoons olive oil	10 to 15 grinds black pepper
1½ cups medium-diced red onion	⅔ cup balsamic vinegar
2 tablespoons minced fresh rosemary	½ cup light brown sugar
3 bay leaves	

Preheat the broiler to high. Place the peppers on a foil-lined baking pan and broil, turning the peppers frequently, until they begin to char, about 15 to 20 minutes. Transfer the peppers to a bowl, and cover it with plastic wrap to steam and loosen the skins. When they're cool enough to handle, peel, seed, and medium dice the peppers. You should have 3 cups. Set the peppers aside.

In a 10-inch sauté pan, stir together the oil, onions, rosemary, bay leaves, allspice, salt, and pepper. Simmer over low heat, stirring occasionally, until the onions are soft and translucent but have not begun to color, about 10 to 15 minutes.

Add the peppers, vinegar, and sugar. Increase the heat and simmer, stirring occasionally, until most of the liquid has evaporated and the mixture looks sticky and gooey, about 20 minutes. The chutney is done when you can drag a large spoon across the bottom of the pan and the mixture holds its shape. Remove and discard the bay leaves.

Wash the jars, lids, and bands in very hot soapy water, rinse them well, and place them upside down on a clean towel to drain.

Spoon the chutney into the jars, leaving a half inch of headroom to allow for expansion during freezing. Wipe the rims with a clean wet cloth or paper towel, add the lids and bands, and finger tighten the bands.

Label the jars. Cool completely before tightening the bands and storing the jars in the refrigerator or freezer.

QUICK IDEAS // Pepper chutney is terrific alongside curries and stirred into yogurt for a sauce to top fish. Mix it into mayonnaise to dress chicken salad and slather onto sandwiches.

radishes

Radishes like growing in cool climates. The long breakfast radishes, tiny globe radishes, soot black radishes with a bone white interior, pure white daikons, and Beauty Heart radishes (aka watermelon radish, named for its look-a-like fruit)—all of them are crunchy and juicy with differing levels of heat. Colorful red radishes make beautiful pickles and are among the easiest vegetables to ferment.

fermented radishes with juniper and coriander

MAKES 1 QUART

This fermented condiment is both flavorful and very pretty. Use a clip-top jar with a rubber gasket to allow the gases to escape as the vegetables ferment. If using a canning jar, loosely screw on the top, making make sure it's not too tight.

2 teaspoons salt

2 cups boiling water, plus more for rinsing the jar

1 pound radishes, sliced very thin (about 4 cups)

1 tablespoon juniper berries

1 tablespoon coriander seeds

2 Fresno peppers, sliced crosswise into thin rings

2-inch piece of ginger, peeled and sliced thin

In a medium bowl, dissolve the salt in 2 cups of boiling water. Set the bowl aside.

Rinse the jar and gasket with boiling water. Pack the radishes, juniper berries, coriander seeds, peppers, and ginger into the jar, and add the brine. Make sure to leave about 1 inch of headroom for expansion as the radishes ferment.

Cover the jar with a double-layer square of wax paper a bit larger than the jar opening, fold in the corners with a clean spoon, and gently push down so some of the brine comes up over the wax paper. This will keep the radishes submerged and oxygen out.

Close the jar, set it on a plate, and let it sit for at least 6 to 8 days before opening. Taste the radishes. The longer the jar sits, the more the vegetables will ferment. Once fermented, refrigerate the radishes.

QUICK IDEAS // Enjoy eating these peppery, tangy radishes straight from the jar! Serve them on a cheese plate, take them on picnics, and chop and fold them into chicken salad.

tomatillos

Tomatillos remind us of green tomatoes, which are their very distant cousin. Tomatillos are actually in the same genus as gooseberries and ground cherries. They're acidic, adding a tangy snap to salsas. Don't peel tomatillos until you're ready to use them: the peel retains the moisture, keeping them fresh. The sticky sap under the papery peel is harmless.

chipotle tomatillo salsa

MAKES ABOUT 4 HALF-PINTS

Searing the tomatillos and garlic gives this spicy salsa a rich, smoky kiss. It's quick and easy to prepare and makes great use of backyard tomatillos. Lining the frying pan with foil cuts the cleaning time in half.

2 pounds tomatillos, husked and cut in half

8 to 12 very large garlic cloves, peeled

2 teaspoons salt

up to 8 canned chipotle peppers in adobo, drained

Line two large frying pans with foil, or work in two batches. Heat the pans over medium heat, put the tomatillos cut side down on the pan, add the garlic, and cook until the tomatillos are soft and brown, about 5 to 10 minutes per side.

Carefully lift the corners of the foil and turn the tomatillos, garlic, and salt into a food processor fitted with a steel blade. Add the chipotle peppers to the processor a couple at a time. Pulse to lightly puree the salsa. If it's too thick, add a little water. Taste, and add more peppers if desired. (We like this salsa hot, so we use about 8 chipotles in a batch.)

Wash the jars, lids, and bands in very hot soapy water, rinse them well, and place them upside down on a clean towel to drain.

Spoon the salsa into the jars, leaving a half inch of headroom to allow for expansion during freezing. Wipe the rims with a clean wet cloth or paper towel, add the lids and bands, and finger tighten the bands.

Label the jars. Cool completely before tightening the bands and storing the jars in the refrigerator or freezer.

QUICK IDEAS // Perfect with chips and an icy cold beer, this easy salsa will perk up burgers, tacos, and burritos. Serve a dollop of it on black bean soup.

spicy tomatillo and lime jam

MAKES ABOUT 3 HALF-PINTS

Tomatillos taste like a puckery cross of a tomato and a lemon. They're tart when raw, fruity when cooked. Slightly underripe tomatillos are a perfect choice here because they're higher in pectin and help create a thick, rich jam.

2 pounds tomatillos, husked and coarsely chopped (about 6 to 7 cups)	1 tablespoon finely grated lime zest
1 cup sugar	½ cup jalapeño peppers, seeded and minced
½ cup water	½ teaspoon salt
½ cup fresh lime juice	

Put a small plate in the freezer for the set test.

Combine all of the ingredients in a 10-inch sauté pan set over medium heat, and bring it to a gentle boil. Lower the heat, and simmer, stirring occasionally, until most of the liquid has evaporated, about 15 to 20 minutes. Remove the pan from the heat and do a set test (page 10). For a thicker jam, return the pan to the heat for a few minutes, and then repeat the test.

Wash the jars, lids, and bands in very hot soapy water, rinse them well, and place them upside down on a clean towel to drain.

Spoon the jam into the jars, leaving a half inch of headroom to allow for expansion during freezing. Wipe the rims with a clean wet cloth or paper towel, add the lids and bands, and finger tighten the bands.

Label the jars. Cool completely before tightening the bands and storing the jars in the refrigerator or freezer.

QUICK IDEAS // Serve this jam on mild, fresh cheese such as ricotta, chèvre, or artisan cream cheese with hard crackers. Try it on a cheese biscuit or a plain scone.

tomatoes

If you grow tomatoes, these quick and easy recipes will capture your hard work and the taste of sunshine in a jar. Make these preserves when the tomatoes are at their peak, whether you've picked them from your garden or the farmers market. Come January, you'll be so happy you did.

oven-dried tomatoes

Our northern summers are way too humid and too short for sun-drying tomatoes, so we rely on the oven. This can take a while, from 4 to 8 hours, depending on the tomatoes and your oven's temperature; play it by ear. Just know that in the dead of winter, your patience will truly pay off. This recipe is supremely simple, and the resulting tomatoes are sublime.

Paste (or Roma) and cherry varieties work best for oven drying. Large slicing tomatoes are too juicy and take far too long.

Because the tomatoes shrink in the heat, it's fine to place them close to each other, regardless of what other recipes suggest. Set the tomatoes cut side up on a parchment-covered mesh wire rack and place that directly on the oven's rack so that air circulates evenly around all sides (parchment keeps the tomatoes from sticking). A convection oven is best for oven drying; with a conventional oven, rotate the tomatoes every hour.

These delicious tomatoes are what we use in our White Bean Dip with Oven-Dried Tomatoes and Smoked Paprika (page 21) and Puttanesca Sauce (page 84).

cherry or paste tomatoes
salt

Preheat the oven to 200 degrees. Wash the tomatoes well, and cut away any blemishes. Line a mesh wire rack with parchment paper. You can use a parchment-lined baking pan instead, but this will increase the drying time.

Cut the tomatoes in half lengthwise (from stem to blossom end), and place them cut side up on the rack. It's OK for the tomatoes to touch; put as many on the rack as you can fit. Generously sprinkle salt on the tomatoes.

Place the rack in the oven. Rotate the rack, or racks if drying on more than one rack, every couple of hours (or every hour if you are using a conventional oven).

continued on next page

The drying time will depend on the types of tomatoes used, your oven, and how dry you want the tomatoes; plan on at least 4 hours.

Let the tomatoes cool complete on the rack, and then place them in freezer bags or canning jars. Store them in the refrigerator or freezer.

QUICK IDEAS // Punchy and flavor-packed, these dried tomatoes are meant to top pizza, toss into pasta, stir into rice, layer into hoagies, and simmer in sauce.

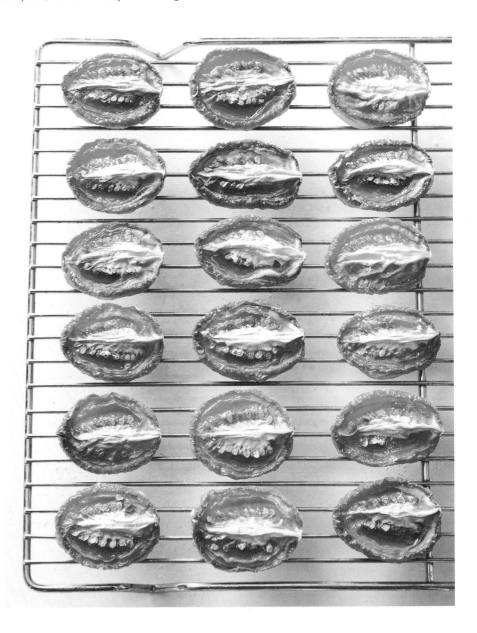

chunky tamarind ketchup

MAKES ABOUT 5 HALF-PINTS

Inspired by the fragrant tamarind-spiced sauces of Thai, Indian, and Caribbean cuisine, this ketchup is more tangy than sweet. The lively, chunky ketchup will have you rethinking your definition of the all-American condiment. You'll find tamarind concentrate in most ethnic grocers and some natural food co-ops.

4 pounds paste (or Roma) tomatoes, medium diced (about 10 cups)

2 cups medium-diced onions

2 tablespoons medium-diced garlic

1 cup tamarind concentrate

½ cup sugar

½ cup cider vinegar

2 teaspoons salt

2 teaspoons ground allspice

½ teaspoon ground cinnamon

½ teaspoon ground cloves

Working in batches, puree the tomatoes in a food processor fitted with a steel blade. Scrape the tomatoes into a medium mesh sieve set over a deep bowl, and let the tomatoes drain for about 15 to 20 minutes. Reserve the liquid. Turn the drained tomatoes into a 10-inch sauté pan.

In a food processor, puree the onions and garlic. Stir the puree into the tomatoes along with a cup of the reserved tomato liquid. Add the tamarind, sugar, vinegar, salt, allspice, cinnamon, and cloves.

Set the pan over medium heat, and bring the ketchup to a gentle boil. Lower the heat, and simmer, uncovered, stirring occasionally, until the mixture thickens; about 15 minutes. The ketchup is done when you can drag a large spoon across the bottom of the pan and the mixture holds its shape.

For a smoother consistency, place a medium mesh sieve over a deep bowl. Working in batches, press the ketchup through the sieve, scraping the underside of the sieve with a clean spoon. Discard the solids left in the sieve.

Wash the jars, lids, and bands in very hot soapy water, rinse them well, and place them upside down on a clean towel to drain.

Spoon the ketchup into the jars, leaving a half inch of headroom to allow for expansion during freezing. Wipe the rims with a clean wet cloth or paper towel, add the lids and bands, and finger tighten the bands.

Label the jars. Cool completely before tightening the bands and storing the jars in the refrigerator or freezer.

QUICK IDEAS // Use this tangy tomato condiment on grilled lamb burgers, chicken, and fish. It's great as the base for a soup or stirred into Greek yogurt or sour cream to top mashed sweet potatoes and roasted vegetables.

curried ketchup with star anise

As this sauce simmers, aromas of curry, anise, and tomatoes will fill your kitchen. It's so good, you'll find yourself eating it from the jar with a spoon. Warning: this may spoil you—now the stuff in a plastic squeeze bottle just won't do.

Try using a mix of different tomatoes—acidic, sweet, and mellow. We tested this recipe with yellow cherry, red paste, and black slicing tomatoes for stunning ketchup.

2 tablespoons olive oil	1 teaspoon salt
1½ cups medium-diced red onions	10 to 15 grinds black pepper
1 tablespoon medium-diced garlic	2 pounds mixed tomatoes, medium diced
⅓ cup sugar	(about 5 cups)
2 star anise	½ cup cider vinegar
2 teaspoons curry powder	

In a 10-inch sauté pan, combine the olive oil, onions, and garlic. Sauté over medium-low heat until the onions are soft and translucent but not browned, about 5 minutes. Add the sugar, star anise, curry powder, salt, and pepper, and cook until the sugar begins to caramelize, another 5 to 10 minutes.

Add the tomatoes and vinegar, and bring to a gentle boil. Lower the heat and simmer, stirring occasionally, until the mixture is thick and most of the liquid has evaporated, about 45 minutes. The ketchup is done when you can drag a large spoon across the bottom of the pan and the mixture holds its shape. Remove and discard the star anise. Taste, and adjust the seasoning.

For a smoother ketchup, place a medium mesh sieve over a deep bowl. Working in batches, press the ketchup through the sieve, scraping the underside of the sieve with a clean spoon. Discard the solids left in the sieve.

Wash the jars, lids, and bands in very hot soapy water, rinse them well, and place them upside down on a clean towel to drain.

Spoon the ketchup into the jars, leaving a half inch of headroom to allow for expansion during freezing. Wipe the rims with a clean wet cloth or paper towel, add the lids and bands, and finger tighten the bands.

Label the jars. Cool completely before tightening the bands and storing the jars in the refrigerator or freezer.

QUICK IDEAS // This ketchup is a must on grilled lamb burgers and lamb sausage. It also makes a great base for a curry soup with coconut milk. Try it with grilled or roasted eggplant, sweet potatoes, and as a dip for pita chips.

puttanesca sauce

MAKES ABOUT 4 PINTS

Spicy, fast, and easy, this is the perfect sauce to have on hand all year long. Make it when you have a glut of tomatoes, and make two batches; it freezes beautifully.

4 pounds paste (or Roma) tomatoes, coarsely chopped (about 11 to 12 cups)

3 tablespoons minced garlic

1 tablespoon minced anchovies (about 1 ounce)

1 teaspoon crushed red pepper flakes

1 tablespoon olive oil

⅔ cup coarsely chopped oven-dried tomatoes (page 79) or ¼ cup coarsely chopped sun-dried tomatoes

1 tablespoon sugar

1 tablespoon white balsamic vinegar

2 teaspoons salt

⅔ cup slivered, pitted, and drained kalamata olives

⅓ cup drained capers (about 1½ ounces)

⅓ cup chopped fresh oregano

1 tablespoon lemon juice

10 to 15 grinds black pepper

Working in batches, pulse the tomatoes a few times in a food processor fitted with a steel blade. Put them in a large bowl.

In a 10-inch sauté pan, stir together the garlic, anchovies, crushed red pepper flakes, and olive oil, and cook over medium heat until the mixture becomes fragrant, about 3 to 4 minutes. Stir in the fresh tomatoes.

Increase the heat, and bring the mixture to a boil. Add the oven-dried tomatoes, sugar, vinegar, and salt. Measure the sauce using the dipstick method (page 9). Lower the heat and simmer, uncovered, stirring occasionally, until the sauce has reduced by almost half, about 35 to 45 minutes. Remove the sauce from the heat, and stir in the olives, capers, oregano, lemon juice, and black pepper.

Wash the jars, lids, and bands in very hot soapy water, rinse them well, and place them upside down on a clean towel to drain.

Spoon the sauce into the jars, leaving a half inch of headroom to allow for expansion during freezing. Wipe the rims with a clean wet cloth or paper towel, add the lids and bands, and finger tighten the bands.

Label the jars. Cool completely before tightening the bands and storing the jars in the refrigerator or freezer.

QUICK IDEAS // This is a great sauce for simmering scallops, shrimp, and chicken. It's terrific tossed with pasta or spread over pizza.

tomato and pepper salsa

MAKES ABOUT 3 OR 4 PINTS

We call this "end of the season salsa." Roasting the tomatoes helps release the liquid and cuts down on the simmering time, resulting in a fresh, lively flavor.

4½ pounds mixed heirloom and paste tomatoes	½ cup finely diced mixed hot peppers
1 tablespoon salt	½ cup cider vinegar
2 cups medium-diced onions	¼ cup lime juice
3 tablespoons minced garlic	½ teaspoon cayenne pepper
1½ cups medium-diced mixed sweet peppers	1 teaspoon crushed red pepper flakes
	1 tablespoon honey (optional)

Preheat the oven to 425 degrees. Trim the stem ends of the tomatoes and any blemishes, cut the tomatoes into large chunks, and place them on two foil-lined baking sheets. Sprinkle with 1½ teaspoons of the salt, and roast for 15 minutes. Drain off the liquid, turn the pans, and continue roasting until the tomatoes are tender, wrinkled, and browned, another 15 to 30 minutes (30 to 45 minutes total). Transfer the roasted tomatoes to a colander placed over a deep bowl and drain thoroughly, reserving the liquid. Using scissors, cut the tomatoes into small pieces.

Put the tomatoes, remaining 1½ teaspoons of salt, onions, garlic, sweet and hot peppers, vinegar, lime juice, cayenne, and crushed red pepper flakes into a 10-inch sauté pan set over medium heat. Simmer until the vegetables soften, adding a little of the tomato liquid if they look dry, about 10 minutes. Adjust the seasoning, and add the honey (if using).

Wash the jars, lids, and bands in very hot soapy water, rinse them well, and place them upside down on a clean towel to drain.

Spoon the salsa into the jars, leaving a half inch of headroom to allow for expansion during freezing. Wipe the rims with a clean wet cloth or paper towel, add the lids and bands, and finger tighten the bands.

Label the jars. Cool completely before tightening the bands and storing the jars in the refrigerator or freezer.

QUICK IDEAS // Add freshly chopped cilantro to this salsa before serving it on tacos, nachos, and burgers and with chips. It's great in black bean and corn salads, terrific on baked potatoes topped with sour cream. Swirl it into corn or fish chowder right before serving.

tomato and apple chutney

MAKES 4 TO 5 HALF-PINTS

This saucy chutney answers those last-minute dinner dilemmas: it has a million uses as a sauce, a condiment, a base for soup. Use a mix of tomatoes for color and flavor. Control the level of heat by varying the amount and type of crushed red pepper flakes and curry.

1½ cups water	1½ teaspoons curry powder
1 tablespoon lime juice	1 teaspoon salt
1 pound tart apples, cored and medium diced (about 3 to 3½ cups)	½ teaspoon crushed red pepper flakes
1 tablespoon olive oil	½ teaspoon ground allspice
1 cup medium-diced onions	¼ teaspoon ground nutmeg
1½ teaspoons minced garlic	1 pound mixed tomatoes, medium diced (about 2½ cups)
¼ cup sugar	¼ cup cider vinegar
1½ teaspoons yellow mustard seeds	¼ cup golden raisins

Put the water and lime juice in a 10-inch sauté pan, and add the apples as they're cut. Over medium-high heat, bring the water to a boil. Reduce to a simmer, cover, and cook until the apples soften but still hold their shape, about 5 minutes. Drain the apples, and set them aside.

In a 10-inch sauté pan, combine the olive oil, onions, and garlic. Cook over medium heat until the onions are soft and translucent but not brown, about 5 to 10 minutes. Stir in the sugar, mustard seeds, curry powder, salt, crushed red pepper flakes, allspice, and nutmeg, and cook until the onions begin to caramelize (but not burn), about 5 minutes.

Add the apples, tomatoes, vinegar, and raisins, and bring the mixture back to a gentle boil. Lower the heat a little and cook, uncovered, stirring occasionally, until most of the liquid has evaporated, about 45 to 60 minutes. Taste, and adjust the seasoning. The chutney is done when you can drag a large spoon across the bottom of the pan and the mixture holds its shape.

Wash the jars, lids, and bands in very hot soapy water, rinse them well, and place them upside down on a clean towel to drain.

Spoon the chutney into the jars, leaving a half inch of headroom to allow for expansion during freezing. Wipe the rims with a clean wet cloth or paper towel, add the lids and bands, and finger tighten the bands.

Label the jars. Cool completely before tightening the bands and storing the jars in the refrigerator or freezer.

QUICK IDEAS // This is a great sauce for poaching fish, chicken, and pork. Serve it alongside curries. Use it as a base for a spicy soup, adding stock and coconut milk to taste.

winter squash

Pickling turned our perception of squash on its head. The pickling process yields crunchy, earthy, delicious pickles and chutney, not the sweet, soft vegetable we're used to serving as a side dish.

squash and apricot chutney

MAKES 5 TO 6 HALF-PINTS

This old-fashioned farmhouse chutney was popular years ago when dried apricots were scarce (and pricey) and the squash from the fields was piled high.

6 ounces dried apricots, cut into small pieces (about 1 cup)

2 teaspoons black peppercorns

1 teaspoon cumin seeds

1 teaspoon coriander seeds

1 pound butternut squash, peeled, seeded, and medium diced (3½ cups)

1 cup medium-diced onions

1 cup cider vinegar

½ cup sugar

2 tablespoons finely grated fresh ginger

1 teaspoon crushed red pepper flakes

½ teaspoon salt

In a small bowl, plump the apricots in 1 cup of water. Cover the bowl and let the apricots soak at least 12 hours or overnight. Drain.

Using a mortar and pestle or a spice mill, lightly crush the peppercorns, cumin, and coriander. Or place the spices in a sealed plastic bag and crush them with a rolling pin or other heavy object.

Put the apricots, ground spices, 1½ cups of water, squash, onions, vinegar, sugar, ginger, crushed red pepper flakes, and salt into a 10-inch sauté pan. Bring the liquid to a boil; then reduce the heat, cover, and simmer to soften the squash, about 10 to 15 minutes. Remove the cover, and continue simmering, stirring occasionally, until the chutney becomes thick and glossy (add a little water if the mixture looks too dry), about 30 minutes. Break up any big pieces of squash using a potato masher or a fork. The chutney is done when you can drag a large spoon across the bottom of the pan and the mixture holds its shape.

Wash the jars, lids, and bands in very hot soapy water, rinse them well, and place them upside down on a clean towel to drain.

Spoon the chutney into the jars, leaving a half inch of headroom to allow for expansion during freezing. Wipe the rims with a clean wet cloth or paper towel, add the lids and bands, and finger tighten the bands.

Label the jars. Cool completely before tightening the bands and storing the jars in the refrigerator or freezer.

QUICK IDEAS // Serve the chutney with feta cheese, grilled or roast lamb, or toasted pita bread (it makes a great dip).

sweet pickled winter squash

MAKES ABOUT 4 HALF-PINTS

This unusual pickle has a fine, firm texture and sweet, zesty flavor. Just right for the Thanksgiving feast!

1 cup cider vinegar	1¼ pounds butternut squash, peeled, seeded, and medium diced (4 cups)
1 cup water	1-inch piece ginger, peeled and thinly sliced
½ cup lime juice	1 teaspoon whole allspice
1 tablespoon finely grated lime zest	1 teaspoon black peppercorns
1 teaspoon crushed red pepper flakes	
½ cup sugar	

In a small saucepan, combine the vinegar, water, lime juice, lime zest, crushed red pepper flakes, and sugar. Bring the mixture to a boil over medium-high heat, stirring to dissolve the sugar. Pour it into a large stainless steel or glass bowl. Add the squash cubes, and mix until the squash is well coated. Cover the bowl, and let the squash macerate at room temperature for 8 hours or overnight.

Drain the liquid from the bowl into a 10-inch sauté pan. Put the ginger, allspice, and peppercorns into a spice bag, or tie them in a square of cheesecloth, and put it in the pan. Over medium-high heat, bring the liquid a boil; then reduce the heat and simmer for 5 minutes. Add the squash, cover, and simmer until the pieces start to turn translucent around the edges and are just softened but firm, about 30 minutes. Remove and discard the spice bag.

Wash the jars, lids, and bands in very hot soapy water, rinse them well, and place them upside down on a clean towel to drain.

Spoon the squash and syrup into the jars, leaving a half inch of headroom to allow for expansion during freezing. Cover each jar with a square of wax paper slightly larger than the jar opening, fold in the corners with a clean spoon, and gently push down so some of the syrup comes up over the wax paper. Wipe the rims with a clean wet cloth or paper towel, add the lids and bands, and finger tighten the bands.

Label the jars. Cool completely before tightening the bands and storing the jars in the refrigerator or freezer.

QUICK IDEAS // This is a terrific condiment for the Thanksgiving turkey and turkey leftovers. It's also great with curries and spiced stews.

zucchini and summer squash

When the zucchini and summer squash take over the garden, put them in a pickle or a relish!

zucchini onion relish

MAKES ABOUT 5 HALF-PINTS

This not-too-sweet relish makes good use of overabundant backyard zucchini.

VEGETABLES
- 1 pound zucchini or yellow summer squash, finely diced (about 3½ cups)
- 1 pound onions, finely diced, about 3 cups
- ½ cup salt

BRINE
- 1½ cups cider vinegar
- ½ cup sugar
- 1 tablespoon yellow mustard seeds
- 5 small sprigs rosemary

Combine the zucchini, onions, and salt in a bowl, and toss well with your fingers. Cover the vegetables with cold water, and set them aside for 1 to 2 hours.

In a 10-inch sauté pan, combine the vinegar, sugar, and mustard seeds. Bring the brine to a gentle boil over medium heat, stirring to dissolve the sugar. Turn off the heat, and let the brine cool.

Pour the vegetables into a colander or a sieve, and rinse them well under cold running water. Drain thoroughly.

Turn the drained vegetables into the sauté pan, and bring the brine to a gentle boil over medium heat. Reduce the heat, and simmer until the vegetables are just softened, about 5 minutes.

Wash the jars, lids, and bands in very hot soapy water, rinse them well, and place them upside down on a clean towel to drain.

Spoon the relish into the jars, leaving a half inch of headroom to allow for expansion during freezing, and place a sprig of rosemary in each jar. Cover each jar with a square of wax paper slightly larger than the jar opening, fold in corners with a clean spoon, and gently push down so some of the brine comes up over the wax paper. Wipe the rims with a clean wet cloth or paper towel, add lids and bands, and finger tighten the bands.

Label the jars. Cool completely before tightening the bands and storing the jars in the refrigerator or freezer.

QUICK IDEAS // Toss this relish into potato salad just before serving. Mix it with mayonnaise for a tartar sauce. Spoon it into sour cream for a dip.

fruit

SHUSH! HERE'S OUR SECRET: these gorgeous jams, chutneys, and conserves, the savory and the sweet, are easy and quick and healthy. Mette is a master of simplicity and restraint. She tastes the food first, then decides how best to showcase its flavor. Never does she load it down with sugar; never is it masked by mouth-searing hot peppers or puckery sour limes. She engages her artist's eye and her taste buds as a guide to deciding what herbs, seasonings, and ingredients need to go into the condiment. It's imprecise, sure, but our grandmothers didn't use measuring cups, and they made a lot of things without much fuss. We've written these recipes to guide you in knowing what to look for as you cook and to fill the kitchen with tempting aromas.

Because these condiments are made in small batches, not big quantities, they cook in far less time than you might expect and their flavors remain fresh. Store them in the refrigerator to enjoy right away (easy to do), or freeze them for later use. They are not shelf stable because they have not been treated to a hot-water bath to seal the jars. We've found that immersing the jars in hot water overcooks the product and dulls the color and punch. This way, the fruits retain their bright gem-like looks.

LEXICON OF FRUIT CONSERVES

The meanings of these terms vary from cook to cook. Here's how we define them:

Jams are made of whole fruit cooked with sugar long enough that the fruit softens into a spread.

Preserves contain whole or big chunks of cooked fruit and are less spreadable than jam.

Fruit butters are smooth and creamy spreads made of long-cooked fruit.

Marmalades are spreads made of whole fruits (most often citrus) and are notably bitter and slightly sweet.

Fresh or frozen? It depends. Top-quality, great-tasting fruit is the key. This doesn't necessarily mean it's the most beautiful. Misshapen strawberries and dented apples (aka seconds) often taste better than the prettiest picks. If you can't get fruit that's super fresh, then flash-frozen fruit is the better choice. How to know what's good enough to preserve? It's all in good taste!

Sugar. We rely on organic evaporated cane sugar. Unlike super-refined white sugar, it has a subtle molasses flavor. And, we know that it's been responsibly sourced, the workers treated well, and the farmers paid a fair price. Our recipes call for less sugar than do most recipes, so our preserves are fruit forward.

Pectin. We don't add pectin to our preserves. Pectin is the carbohydrate that's concentrated in the skin and the seeds of the fruit. When combined with the proper ratio of sugar and acid, pectin causes liquids to jell. Pectin levels vary greatly (even within a single type of fruit), depending on ripeness: pectin content diminishes as fruit matures. The more tart-tasting the fruit, the higher the pectin content will be, so apples and citrus fruits contain a high percentage of pectin.

All of the recipes in this book take advantage of natural fruit pectin. We encourage you to accept the glorious and imperfect nature of home preserves; their vibrant, straightforward flavors tell all.

Macerating the fruit. In this process, sugar and fruit are combined and left to stand several hours or overnight. The sugar draws out the fruit's juices and so shortens the cooking time to yield a fresher-tasting product.

Extracting juice from cooked fruit. What's the best way to extract juice from cooked fruits? Turn the mass into a colander lined with a clean (cheap) towel or cheesecloth and set over a deep bowl. Allow the cooked fruit to cool a little and then give it a good, hard squeeze. While the juice will be a bit cloudy, you will end up extracting lots of juice quickly. (If you prefer a perfectly clear juice, allow the liquid to drip through the towel in its own time.)

Acidified water. Apples and pears tend to discolor once they're cut. To keep this from happening, we recommend holding the sliced fruit in acidified water—a simple ratio of 1 cup of water to 1 tablespoon of lemon or lime juice. Drain before using the fruit.

apples

The more varied the apples, the more interesting the applesauce and apple butter will be. Because apples cook down beautifully, there's little reason to puree a sauce. If you use a range of sweet, tart apples, there may be no need for sugar at all.

Apples act as a base for a wide variety of preserves, savory and sweet. Tangy, firm, juicy apples are naturally loaded with pectin that thickens the preserves so they'll hold their shape.

applesauce with grapefruit and cardamom

MAKES 4 TO 5 HALF-PINTS

Cardamom is the go-to spice in Nordic kitchens, far more popular than cinnamon. It's the spice the Vikings brought back from Constantinople and, like pepper, was literally worth its weight in gold. Aromatic, citrusy, and slightly herbal, cardamom offers flavor that runs toward the cooler end of the spice spectrum, so it is especially good with tart fruit.

This recipe comes together quickly because there's no need to peel or core the apples. They'll be passed through a sieve after they're cooked. A few crab apples will give the sauce a lovely pinkish hue and tart flavor. For variety, try substituting lime, orange, or lemon for the grapefruit and rosemary, fennel, or sage for the cardamom.

3 pounds apples, coarsely chopped (about 10 cups) and held in acidified water (page 95)

¼ cup water

1 tablespoon cardamom pods, lightly crushed

½ cup fresh grapefruit juice

1 tablespoon finely grated grapefruit zest

sugar to taste

Drain the apples, and put them in a 10-inch sauté pan, along with the water, cardamom pods, grapefruit juice, and zest. Bring the liquid to a boil over medium-high heat; then lower the heat and cover the pan. Simmer the apples, stirring occasionally, until they are very soft, about 20 minutes.

Place a medium mesh sieve over a deep bowl. Working in batches, press the apple mixture through the sieve, occasionally scraping the underside of the sieve with a clean spoon. Discard the solids left in the sieve.

You should have about 4 cups of apple pulp, depending on the variety and juiciness of the apples.

Sweeten the sauce to taste, adding about ¼ cup of sugar (or less) at a time. Put the applesauce in the pan, return it to the stove, and dissolve the sugar over low heat.

Wash the jars, lids, and bands in very hot soapy water, rinse them well, and place them upside down on a clean towel to drain.

Spoon the applesauce into the jars, leaving a half inch of headroom to allow for expansion during freezing. Wipe the rims with a clean wet cloth or paper towel, add the lids and bands, and finger tighten the bands.

Label the jars. Cool completely and tighten the bands before storing the jars in the refrigerator or freezer.

QUICK IDEAS // Make an applesauce granita by turning the sauce into a metal bowl and setting it in the freezer, stirring occasionally, until the sauce is nearly frozen. Serve the granita with a dollop of freshly whipped cream. Applesauce is a natural with roast pork, lamb, and chicken, and is terrific on vanilla ice cream or yogurt.

caramel apple butter with lemongrass

MAKES 3 TO 4 HALF-PINTS

The soft, lemony flavor of lemongrass enriches this lush, caramel-colored apple butter. You can spread it on toast or scones; we eat it right from the jar. No need to peel and core the apples—they'll come out when the cooked apples are passed through a sieve. This makes a terrific gift.

- 3 pounds apples, coarsely chopped (about 10 cups) and held in acidified water (page 95)
- 2 cups unsweetened apple juice
- 1 cup packed light brown sugar
- 3 tablespoons champagne vinegar
- 2 (5-inch) pieces lemongrass, slightly crushed
- ½ teaspoon ground cinnamon

Drain the apples, put them in a 10-inch sauté pan, and add the apple juice. Bring the liquid to a boil over medium-high heat; then lower the heat and cover the pan. Simmer the apples, stirring occasionally, until they're very soft, about 20 minutes.

Place a medium mesh sieve over a deep bowl. Working in batches, press the apple mixture through the sieve, occasionally scraping the underside of the sieve with a clean spoon. Discard the solids left in the sieve.

You should have about 4 cups of apple pulp, depending on the variety and juiciness of the apples.

Clean the pan, and return the apple pulp to the pan. Add the brown sugar, vinegar, lemongrass, and cinnamon. Bring the apple butter to a gentle boil over medium-low heat; then reduce the heat to very low. Simmer uncovered, stirring occasionally, until the apple butter is thick and mounds when placed on a plate, at least 1 hour. Discard the lemongrass pieces.

Wash the jars, lids, and bands in very hot soapy water, rinse them well, and place them upside down on a clean towel to drain.

Spoon the apple butter into the jars, leaving a half inch of headroom to allow for expansion during freezing. Wipe the rims with a clean wet cloth or paper towel, add the lids and bands, and finger tighten the bands.

Label the jars. Cool completely and tighten the bands before storing the jars in the refrigerator or freezer.

QUICK IDEAS // Apple butter is especially good on plain scones and sliced pound cake and swirled into plain yogurt. Fill pastry shells and cookie cups with apple butter and top it with whipped cream.

earl grey crab apple jelly

MAKES 3 TO 4 HALF-PINTS

Crab apple trees grow beautifully along the northern shores of Lake Superior, as they do throughout all northern climates. Bees love their gorgeous white and pink blossoms that make the hillsides appear covered in snow. The small, tart fruits make an exquisite, rose-colored jelly. This jelly's subtle notes of bergamot, provided by Earl Grey tea, will keep people guessing.

1½ tablespoons loose-leaf Earl Grey tea
½ cup boiling water
3 pounds crab apples, halved and held in acidified water (page 95)

1½ cups sugar
2 tablespoons lime juice

Make a strong tea by putting the tea leaves into the boiling water. Steep for 15 minutes; then strain out and discard the leaves. You should have about ⅓ cup of tea. Set the tea aside.

Drain the crab apples, put them into a 10-inch sauté pan, and add enough cold water to just cover the fruit. Bring the water to a simmer over medium heat, and cook, stirring and mashing occasionally, until the crab apples are very soft, about 20 minutes.

Place a colander lined with a clean towel or cheesecloth over a deep bowl, add the crab apple pulp, and let the juice strain for at least 4 hours or overnight. (Do not be tempted to squeeze the pulp, because the juice will turn cloudy.) Discard the pulp. Measure the juice; you should have about 4 cups. If you have a different amount, adjust the sugar level accordingly.

Place a small plate in the freezer. In a 10-inch sauté pan, combine the crab apple juice, sugar, and lime juice. Bring the liquid to a gentle boil over medium heat. Cook uncovered at a low boil, skimming off any foam that rises to the surface and stirring occasionally to prevent sticking, about 20 minutes. Add the tea, and continue cooking another 3 to 5 minutes.

Remove the pan from the heat, and do a set test (page 10). If the jelly isn't thick enough, return the pan to the heat for a few minutes, and then repeat the test.

Wash the jars, lids, and bands in very hot soapy water, rinse them well, and place them upside down on a clean towel to drain.

Pour the jelly into the jars, leaving a half inch of headroom to allow for expansion during freezing. Wipe the rims with a clean wet cloth or paper towel, add the lids and bands, and finger tighten the bands.

Label the jars. Cool completely and tighten the bands before storing the jars in the refrigerator or freezer.

QUICK IDEAS // This jelly makes a wonderful glaze for lamb, chicken, and pork. Whisk a little into a vinaigrette. Spread it on a turkey or ham sandwich. It's terrific on toast and scones.

oven-dried apples

Apples are the easiest and most satisfying fruits to dry. Great for snacking, they're also perfect for adding to trail mix. If you have a mandoline, here's the place to use it. The thinner the apple slices, the more beautifully and evenly they'll dry. The quickest method is to place the apple slices on parchment-lined mesh wire racks so that air circulates evenly around all sides. The parchment keeps the apple slices from sticking. Baking sheets will work too, but the drying time will be much longer.

Preheat the oven to 200 degrees; set convection ovens to 175 degrees. Line one or more mesh wire racks with parchment paper.

Prepare some acidified water. The amount you need will depend on the amount of apples you're prepping. Use a ratio of 1 cup of water to 1 tablespoon of lemon juice. Core the apples, remove the ends, and slice as thinly as possible using a mandoline or a very sharp knife. If you're cutting by hand, halve the apples before slicing for easier handling. Toss the apple slices into the acidified water.

Drain the apple slices, and pat them dry with a clean kitchen towel. Place the apple slices as close together on the lined racks as possible without overlapping. Place the racks of apple slices directly on the oven racks. Bake the apple slices until they are very dry, rotating the racks occasionally to ensure even drying. It will take 2 to 3 hours, depending on the apple variety and how dry you prefer the apples. Cool the slices, and store them in large canning jars in the refrigerator or freezer.

QUICK IDEAS // Toss dried apples into cake, cookie, and muffin batters. The slices make a pretty garnish on salads and pumpkin or squash soup. Toss them with raisins and nuts for a trail mix.

savory apple compote with horseradish and chili

MAKES ABOUT 5 HALF-PINTS

This chunky, fiery compote is versatile and quick to prepare. Thanks to horseradish's natural bacterial qualities, this compote will keep several months in the refrigerator. It's a wonderful autumn side dish when apples are in their prime.

3 pounds tart apples, peeled, cored, and coarsely chopped (about 9 cups), held in acidified water (page 95)

¼ cup water

¾ cup sugar

3 to 4 tablespoons finely grated fresh horseradish (see note)

2 teaspoons crushed red pepper flakes

Drain the apples. Put the apples and the ¼ cup of water into a 10-inch sauté pan set over medium heat. Bring the mixure to a gentle boil; then reduce to a simmer and cover. Cook, stirring occasionally, until the apples are soft, about 8 to 10 minutes. Mash the cooked apples with a fork for a rough, chunky texture.

Stir in the sugar, horseradish, and crushed red pepper flakes. Simmer, uncovered, stirring, until the sugar is dissolved, about 3 minutes.

Wash the jars, lids, and bands in very hot soapy water, rinse them well, and place them upside down on a clean towel to drain.

Spoon the compote into the jars, leaving a half inch of headroom to allow for expansion during freezing. Wipe the rims with a clean wet cloth or paper towel, add the lids and bands, and finger tighten the bands.

Label the jars. Cool completely and tighten the bands before storing the jars in the refrigerator or freezer.

NOTE: If using fresh horseradish, grate it immediately before adding it to the apple compote. When exposed to air, fresh horseradish discolors quickly and its fiery taste intensifies.

QUICK IDEAS // Serve the compote with strong cheeses, cured and smoked meats, and ham. It's great mixed with mayonnaise for a sandwich spread.

blackberries

With their complex floral flavor, blackberries make a lush, rich conserve. Unless you have backyard canes, blackberries are best sourced from the farmers market or a nearby farm. If not farm fresh, frozen berries are your next best choice.

blackberry bay jam

MAKES ABOUT 4 HALF-PINTS

We love the gentle flavor of Meyer lemons in this recipe. Meyer lemons are sweeter and less acidic than other lemons. If they're not available, go ahead and use the more common varieties. Just increase the amount of sugar to taste. This is a bold savory-sweet jam with endless possibilities.

3 pounds blackberries (about 9 cups)
1 cup sugar
¼ cup fresh Meyer lemon juice
1 tablespoon finely grated Meyer lemon zest
3 bay leaves

Combine all of the ingredients in a 10-inch sauté pan. Cover the pan, and let the fruit macerate at room temperature for at least 2 hours or overnight.

Put a small plate in the freezer for the set test. Uncover the pan, and set it over medium-high heat. Bring the liquid to a gentle boil; then lower the heat and simmer, stirring occasionally, until the liquid is nearly evapoated and the jam thickens, about 15 to 20 minutes. If the mixture looks too dry, add a little water. After about 10 minutes of cooking, mash the blackberries with a potato masher or a fork to make a smoother jam. Remove and discard the bay leaves.

Remove the pan from the heat and do a set test (page 10). If the jam isn't thick enough, return the pan to the heat for a few minutes, and then repeat the test.

Wash the jars, lids, and bands in very hot soapy water, rinse them well, and place them upside down on a clean towel to drain.

Spoon the jam into the jars, leaving a half inch of headroom to allow for expansion during freezing. Wipe the rims with a clean wet cloth or paper towel, add the lids and bands, and finger tighten the bands.

Label the jars. Cool completely and tighten the bands before storing the jars in the refrigerator or freezer.

QUICK IDEAS // Try whisking the jam into a vinaigrette or mayonnaise. Create a glaze for chicken or pork by mixing it with a dab of mustard. For breakfast, swirl the jam into plain yogurt and top it with granola.

blackberry preserves with lime and candied ginger

This is such a quick, easy recipe, you'll find yourself making it for last-minute gifts.

3 pounds blackberries (about 9 cups)

1½ cups sugar

2 tablespoons fresh lime juice

1 tablespoon minced Candied Ginger (page 171)

1 tablespoon finely grated lime zest

Combine all the ingredients in a 10-inch sauté pan. Cover the pan and let the fruit macerate at room temperature for least 2 hours or overnight.

Place a small plate in the freezer for the set test. Uncover the pan, and set it over medium-high heat. Bring the liquid to a gentle boil; then lower the heat and simmer, stirring occasionally and carefully so as not to break the berries, until most of the liquid has evaporated, about 15 to 20 minutes.

Remove the pan from the heat and do a set test (page 10). If the preserves aren't thick enough, return the pan to the heat for a few minutes, and then repeat the test.

Wash the jars, lids, and bands in very hot soapy water, rinse them well, and place them upside down on a clean towel to drain.

Spoon the preserves into the jars, leaving a half inch of headroom to allow for expansion during freezing. Wipe the rims with a clean wet cloth or paper towel, add the lids and bands, and finger tighten the bands.

Label the jars. Cool completely and tighten the bands before storing the jars in the refrigerator or freezer.

QUICK IDEAS // We love this preserve over vanilla ice cream and lemon sorbet. It makes a terrific filling for open-faced tarts and thumbprint cookies.

blackberry syrup with lime and lemongrass

MAKES 4 HALF-PINTS

Keep this syrup on hand! The color is gorgeous, and the flavor is intense. It can be used in a fast, refreshing drink and a pretty glaze.

3 pounds blackberries (about 9 cups)

½ cup water

2 (5-inch) pieces lemongrass, slightly crushed

1 cup sugar

1 vanilla bean, split in half lengthwise

2 tablespoons champagne vinegar

1 tablespoon finely grated lime zest

2 tablespoons fresh lime juice

Put the blackberries, water, and lemongrass into a 10-inch sauté pan. Set the heat to medium-high, and bring the mixture to a gentle boil. Reduce the heat to simmer, cover, and cook until the berries are very soft and have released their juices, about 10 minutes.

Place a colander lined with a clean towel or cheesecloth over a deep bowl. Pour in the fruit mixture, and let it strain for at least 2 hours. Gather the corners of the cloth and squeeze to release more juice, scraping the underside of the cloth with a spoon. Discard the fruit pulp left in the cloth. Measure the juice: you should have about 4 cups. If you don't, adjust the amount of sugar to taste.

Clean the sauté pan, pour in the juice, and add the sugar, vanilla bean, vinegar, lime zest, and lime juice. Measure the depth of the syrup with the dipstick method (page 9). Bring the liquid to a boil over medium-high heat; then lower the heat to a simmer. Cook, uncovered, stirring occasionally and skimming off any foam that forms on the top. Simmer until the syrup has reduced by a third, about 15 minutes. (For a thicker syrup, reduce by half, about 30 minutes.) Remove and discard the vanilla bean.

Wash the jars, lids, and bands in very hot soapy water, rinse them well, and place them upside down on a clean towel to drain.

Spoon the syrup into the jars, leaving a half inch of headroom to allow for expansion during freezing. Wipe the rims with a clean wet cloth or paper towel, add the lids and bands, and finger tighten the bands.

Label the jars. Cool completely and tighten the bands before storing the jars in the refrigerator or freezer.

....

QUICK IDEAS // Whisk this syrup into vinaigrettes. Brush it over chicken or pork as a glaze. Make a refreshing drink by mixing it with sparkling water; add a splash of vodka or rum for a great cocktail.

blueberries

Tiny, dark, and intensely flavored, wild blueberries grow in abundance across the north-land. We gather them on the North Shore, eating as many as we put in our pails. Among the cultivated varieties, the darker berries are tastier and more nutritious.

fit for a queen jam

MAKES ABOUT 2 HALF-PINTS

Inspired by an old Swedish recipe, this beautiful jam—equal parts raspberries and blue-berries—is certainly fit for a queen. We've cut back on the sugar and added a touch of mint to our version. You can also make this with frozen fruit; just know that it will be a bit runnier.

½ pound raspberries (about 2 cups)
½ pound blueberries (about 2 cups)
¾ cup sugar
¼ cup water

2 tablespoons lemon juice
2 large sprigs mint, preferably orange mint
    or another fragrant variety

Place a small plate in the freezer for the set test. Combine all the ingredients in a 10-inch sauté pan set over medium-high heat. Bring the mixture to a gentle boil; then lower the heat to a slow simmer. Cook, uncovered and stirring occasionally, until the mixture thickens, about 10 minutes. Remove and discard the mint sprigs.

Remove the pan from the heat, and do a set test (page 10). If the jam isn't thick enough, return the pan to the heat for a few minutes, and then repeat the test.

Wash the jars, lids, and bands in very hot soapy water, rinse them well, and place them upside down on a clean towel to drain.

Spoon the jam into the jars, leaving a half inch of headroom to allow for expansion during freezing. Wipe the rims with a clean wet cloth or paper towel, add the lids and bands, and finger tighten the bands.

Label the jars. Cool completely and tighten the bands before storing the jars in the refrigerator or freezer.

QUICK IDEAS // Layer this jam into muffin and cake batter, and use it to fill pastry shells. Whip it with cream to dollop onto slices of pound cake. It's great in thumbprint cookies and linzer bars.

savory blueberry jam with rosemary, black pepper, and lemon verbena

MAKES ABOUT 3 HALF-PINTS

Black pepper punches up the musky notes of blueberry, while the lemon verbena adds a mellow, lemony touch.

2 pounds blueberries (about 7 cups)

¼ cup water

½ cup sugar

2 tablespoons white wine vinegar

3 large sprigs rosemary

2 large sprigs lemon verbena

1 teaspoon finely ground black pepper

Place a small plate in the freezer for the set test. Combine all the ingredients in a 10-inch sauté pan set over medium-high heat. Bring the liquid to a gentle boil; then lower the heat to a simmer. Cook, stirring occasionally and skimming off any foam that forms on the surface. Mash the berries with the back of a fork for a smoother jam. Simmer until the mixture thickens, about 10 to 15 minutes.

Remove the pan from the heat, and do a set test (page 10). If the jam isn't thick enough, return the pan to the heat for a few minutes, and then repeat the test. Remove and discard the herbs.

Wash the jars, lids, and bands in very hot soapy water, rinse them well, and place them upside down on a clean towel to drain.

Spoon the jam into the jars, leaving a half inch of headroom to allow for expansion during freezing. Wipe the rims with a clean wet cloth or paper towel, add the lids and bands, and finger tighten the bands.

Label the jars. Cool completely and tighten the bands before storing the jars in the refrigerator or freezer.

QUICK IDEAS // This lively jam will brighten a cheese plate and a savory cheesecake. Whisk it into mayonnaise to dress a turkey salad garnished with dried blueberries and nuts.

sweet blueberry vinegar

MAKES ABOUT 2 HALF-PINTS

You can purchase lovely fruit vinegars in specialty stores, but it's so easy to make your own, why pay the price? This recipe works for just about any berry, so mix them up! Because vinegar is so high in acid, it will keep indefinitely in the refrigerator; there's no need to freeze it.

1 pound blueberries (3 to 4 cups)
1 cup white wine vinegar
¾ cup sugar

Combine the blueberries and vinegar in a glass or stainless steel bowl. Use a potato masher or a fork to crush the fruit and release the juices. Cover the bowl tightly, and leave it on the kitchen counter, out of direct sunlight, for 5 days.

Place a medium mesh sieve over a deep bowl, pour in the fruit mixture, and let it strain until no more liquid runs out. Discard the solids. You should have about 1 cup of juice.

Turn the blueberry vinegar into a small saucepan, add the sugar, and bring the vinegar to a gentle boil over medium-high heat. Lower the heat and simmer, stirring, until the sugar dissolves, about 5 minutes.

Wash the jars, lids, and bands in very hot soapy water, rinse them well, and place them upside down on a clean towel to drain.

Pour the vinegar into the jars. Wipe the rims with a clean wet cloth or paper towel, add the lids and bands, and finger tighten the bands.

Label the jars. Cool completely and tighten the bands before storing the jars in the refrigerator.

QUICK IDEAS // Drizzle a little sweet-tangy vinegar over sliced peaches to give contrasting color and tang. Make a refreshing drink by adding a generous shot to a glass of soda water: serve garnished with a few blueberries.

cherries

Most of the cherries that grow in the northland are the hardy tart varieties, but a few orchards are also harvesting sweeter fruit. Tart cherries give an almond-rich flavor to conserves. In all of these recipes, frozen cherries work as well as fresh cherries.

It's almost impossible to remove all the pits. Once the fruit is cooked and split, the pits will float to the surface where they're much easier to skim off.

tart cherry jam with vanilla, almond, and star anise

MAKES 3 TO 4 HALF-PINTS

There is a lot going on in this jam, so feel free to alter the ingredients. You can omit the star anise, almond, or vanilla, but together they create a holy trinity of flavor.

2 pounds tart cherries, pitted and coarsely chopped (about 8 cups)

1¾ cups sugar

2 tablespoons vanilla extract

1 tablespoon almond extract

2 star anise

¼ cup lemon juice

Combine the cherries and sugar in a 10-inch sauté pan. Cover the pan, and let the fruit macerate at room temperature for at least 4 hours or overnight.

Put a small plate in the freezer for a set test. Stir the vanilla and almond extracts, star anise, and lemon juice into the fruit, and bring it to a gentle boil over medium-high heat. Lower the heat and simmer, uncovered and stirring occasionally, until the juices have started to evaporate, about 30 minutes. Remove and discard the star anise. Remove the pan from the heat, and do a set test (page 10). If the jam isn't thick enough, return the pan to the heat for a few minutes, and then repeat the test.

Wash the jars, lids, and bands in very hot soapy water, rinse them well, and place them upside down on a clean towel to drain.

Spoon the jam into the jars, leaving a half inch of headroom to allow for expansion during freezing. Wipe the rims with a clean wet cloth or paper towel, add the lids and bands, and finger tighten the bands.

Label the jars. Cool completely and tighten the bands before storing the jars in the refrigerator or freezer.

QUICK IDEAS // This intensely flavored jam is great served on chèvre or any fresh soft cheese. Use it as a filling in layer cakes, tarts, muffins, and thumbprint cookies. Top off a cheesecake. Whip it into buttercream frosting.

tart cherry syrup with cardamom and black pepper

MAKES 2 TO 3 HALF-PINTS

Cardamom and cherries are a classic Nordic combo; black pepper adds a dash of heat. There is no need to pit the cherries; they will be strained out when you extract the juice.

2 pounds tart cherries, not pitted (about 9 to 10 cups)

2 cups water

⅔ cup sugar

¼ cup cider vinegar

2 tablespoons black peppercorns, crushed

2 tablespoons cardamom pods, crushed

Combine the cherries and the water in a 10-inch sauté pan set over medium-high heat. Bring the water to a gentle boil; then reduce it to a simmer. Cook, covered, stirring occasionally, until the fruit is very soft, about 15 to 20 minutes.

Place a colander lined with a clean towel or cheesecloth over a deep bowl. Turn the cherries into the colander, and let them strain for at least 2 hours or overnight.

Gather the corners of the towel together and squeeze to extract the juice, scraping the outside of the towel with a clean spoon. The juice may appear cloudy, but that will not affect the resulting dark syrup. Discard the solids left in the cloth.

Measure the juice. You should have about 4 cups. For every 2 cups of juice, you will need ⅓ cup sugar and 2 tablespoons vinegar.

Turn the juice, sugar, vinegar, peppercorns, and cardamom into a 10-inch sauté pan and check the depth using the dipstick method (page 9). Bring the juice to a gentle boil over medium-high heat; then lower the heat. Simmer, uncovered, until the juice has reduced by half, about 20 to 30 minutes. Taste the syrup, and adjust the seasoning.

Wash the jars, lids, and bands in very hot soapy water, rinse them well, and place them upside down on a clean towel to drain.

Pour the syrup into the jars, leaving a half inch of headroom to allow for expansion during freezing. Wipe the rims with a clean wet cloth or paper towel, add the lids and bands, and finger tighten the bands.

Label the jars. Cool completely and tighten the bands before storing the jars in the refrigerator or freezer.

QUICK IDEAS // Stir the syrup into soda water or ginger ale for a refreshing drink. Spike that drink with vodka or rum for a winning cocktail. Whisk the syrup into a vinaigrette. Drizzle it over vanilla ice cream, orange sorbet, or a traditional rice pudding.

sweet and savory pickled tart cherries

MAKES 5 HALF-PINTS

Pickled fruit is a traditional condiment throughout the Nordic countries. The acidity in the vinegar balances out the sweetness in the fruit. This pickle's tangy flavor works wonders with a variety of grilled and smoked meats and cheeses. You can use fresh or frozen cherries. Pickled cherries will keep beautifully in the refrigerator for months; there's no need to freeze them.

½ to ¾ cup cherry juice (see note)

½ cup water

½ cup white wine vinegar

½ cup sugar

2 teaspoons pink peppercorns

1 tablespoon finely grated fresh ginger

5 bay leaves

2 pounds tart cherries, pitted (about 8 cups)

Combine the cherry juice, water, vinegar, sugar, peppercorns, ginger, and bay leaves in a 10-inch sauté pan. Turn the heat to medium-high, and bring the liquid to a gentle boil. Reduce the heat, and simmer for several minutes. Turn off the heat, and let the brine rest for 15 minutes.

Wash the jars, lids, and bands in very hot soapy water, rinse them well, and place them upside down on a clean towel to drain.

Divide the cherries between the jars and fill the jars with the brine, distributing the bay leaves and spices among the jars. Cover each jar with a square of wax paper slightly larger than the jar opening, fold in the corners with a clean spoon, and push down gently so some of the brine comes up over the wax paper. Wipe the rims with a clean wet cloth or paper towel, add the lids and bands, and finger tighten the bands.

Label the jars. Cool completely and tighten the bands before storing the jars in the refrigerator. Let the cherries rest for a couple of weeks in the refrigerator to allow the flavors to marry.

NOTE: Collect the juices from fresh cherries by pitting them over a bowl, or thaw frozen cherries in a large bowl and retain the juice. Use the juice in the recipe, adding water if necessary to reach the specified amount.

QUICK IDEAS // Serve the cherries on grilled turkey burgers and sausages, alongside cheese plates, and with curry. Fold them into a chicken salad or put a dollop on top of open-faced grilled cheese sandwiches.

tart cherry compote with ginger, fennel, and bay leaves

MAKES ABOUT 4 HALF-PINTS

Tart cherries get a boost from the medley of ginger, fennel, and bay leaves. The rice vinegar adds a very mild acid touch. We use this boldly flavored, interesting compote on a range of appetizers, grilled chicken, and desserts.

2 pounds tart cherries (about 9 to 10 cups)	2 teaspoons ground ginger
1 cup sugar	2 teaspoons ground fennel (see note)
1 cup water	3 bay leaves
2 tablespoons rice vinegar	½ teaspoon finely ground black pepper

Working over a 10-inch sauté pan, pit the cherries and then cut them with a scissors. This is a great way to make sure you collect all their juices. Stir in the sugar, cover the pan, and let the fruit macerate at room temperature for at least 4 hours or overnight.

Add the water, vinegar, ginger, fennel, bay leaves, and pepper to the sauté pan, and bring the compote to a gentle boil over medium-high heat. Lower the heat and simmer, uncovered and stirring occasionally, until most of the liquid has evaporated, about 30 minutes. Discard the bay leaves.

Wash the jars, lids, and bands in very hot soapy water, rinse them well, and place them upside down on a clean towel to drain.

Spoon the compote into the jars, leaving a half inch of headroom to allow for expansion during freezing. Wipe the rims with a clean wet cloth or paper towel, add the lids and bands, and finger tighten the bands.

Label the jars. Cool completely and tighten the bands before storing the jars in the refrigerator or freezer.

NOTE: If ground fennel is not available, grind fennel seeds with a spice grinder or a mortar and pestle.

QUICK IDEAS // This vibrant condiment stands up to strong cheeses and smoked meats on a charcuterie board. It's great over cream cheese or chèvre with crackers or bruschetta.

citrus

Yes, we know. We don't grow citrus here in the northern tier. But it's played a huge role in our culinary history. No wonder! Sunny, sweet and sour, sometimes bitter, citrus conserves lift the rich, hearty, satisfying roasts, braises, and stews of winter. And they brighten our spirits too.

In marmalades and other recipes where the citrus rind is a primary ingredient, it's important to use organic fruit. Not only is it free from chemicals; it has a cleaner, brighter flavor.

blood orange marmalade
with vanilla and chili

MAKES 5 TO 6 HALF-PINTS

Every year, different varieties of blood oranges (from shades of pink to pure ruby red) come to market. All make a lovely marmalade. This one is vanilla scented and packs a chili kick. It's nearly impossible to get all of the seeds out of these oranges before you put them into the pan, but the seeds will float to the surface as the marmalade simmers and can be easily skimmed off.

2 pounds organic blood oranges

4 cups water

1½ cups sugar

1 vanilla bean

1 teaspoon crushed red pepper flakes

Scrub the oranges well under running water, and remove the hard blossom ends and any blemishes on the skin. Cut the fruit in half lengthwise, and then slice it crosswise into very thin half-moons. Remove and discard seeds as you go.

Put the orange slices in a 10-inch sauté pan with the water. Cover the pan, and macerate the fruit at room temperature for 8 to 24 hours.

Place a small plate in the freezer for the set test. Split the vanilla bean lengthwise, and scrape the seeds into the oranges. Add the vanilla bean and the crushed red pepper flakes to the pan. Bring the marmalade to a gentle boil over medium-high heat, lower the heat, and cover the pan. Simmer, stirring occasionally, for about 30 minutes.

Stir in the sugar and continue simmering, uncovered and stirring occasionally, until the mixture looks sticky and thick, about 45 minutes. Remove the pan from the heat and discard the vanilla bean. Do a set test (page 10). If the marmalade isn't thick enough, return the pan to the heat for a few minutes, and then repeat the test.

Wash the jars, lids, and bands in very hot soapy water, rinse them well, and place them upside down on a clean towel to drain.

Spoon the marmalade into the jars, leaving a half inch of headroom to allow for expansion during freezing. Wipe the rims with a clean wet cloth or paper towel, add the lids and bands, and finger tighten the bands.

Label the jars. Cool completely and tighten the bands before storing the jars in the refrigerator or freezer.

QUICK IDEAS // This marmalade is delicious whisked into plain yogurt to be drizzled over sliced fruit. Mix it with a little coarse mustard to glaze ham or smoked pork chops. Brush it over roasted sweet potatoes or carrots as they come from the oven.

preserved limes with bay leaves and coriander

The initial purpose of preserving citrus fruit in salt and its own juice was to make the precious winter fruit last all year long. Preserving citrus fruits mellows their bold flavor and heightens their citrusy essence. It's the rind of preserved citrus, not the pulp or juice, that's prized. It's delicious in numerous dishes and makes a terrific condiment on its own.

1 pound organic limes	2 teaspoons coriander seeds
¾ cup salt	2 teaspoons black peppercorns
4 bay leaves	1 cup fresh or bottled lime juice

Scrub the limes well, and quarter them lengthwise. Place the salt in a medium bowl, add the lime wedges, and massage the salt into all the surfaces of the lime wedges.

Wash the jar, lid, and band in very hot soapy water, rinse them well, and place them upside down on a clean towel to drain.

Pack the lime wedges in the jar, tucking in the bay leaves and spices. Scrape the salt from the bowl and add it to the jar. Top off the jar with the lime juice. Wipe the rim with a clean wet cloth or paper towel, add the lid, and tighten the band.

Label the jar. Store the jar in the refrigerator. Let the limes cure for at least 1 month before using. The limes will keep for at least 6 months.

QUICK IDEAS // To use the limes, rinse them, remove and discard the pulp, and chop the rind. Toss the rind into farro, barley, and rice salads. It's wonderful added to chickpea stew, stirred into hummus, used as a garnish for curry, and served on grilled chicken.

classic orange marmalade

MAKES 4 TO 5 HALF-PINTS

This variation on classic marmalade calls for common navel oranges and grapefruit juice to create the bitter kick of traditional Seville oranges. The flavors are more tart than sweet, but you can adjust the sugar to taste. Add a little cardamom, ginger, or rosemary for intrigue.

2	pounds organic navel oranges or other sweet oranges	1½	cups sugar
		¾	cup fresh grapefruit juice

Scrub the oranges under running water, and put them into a large pot with 10 cups of water. Set the pot over medium-high heat, and bring it to a gentle boil. Cover the pot, and cook the oranges until they are easily pierced with a sharp knife, about 60 minutes, depending on the size of the fruit. Remove the oranges with tongs and place them on a cutting board. Reserve 4 cups of the cooking water.

When they're cool enough to handle, cut the oranges in half lengthwise. Remove the hard ends and seeds, and slice the orange halves crosswise into very thin half-moons.

Put a plate in the freezer for the set test.

Place the orange slices into a 10-inch sauté pan with the reserved cooking liquid, grapefruit juice, and sugar. Set the pan over medium-high heat, and bring the liquid to a gentle boil. Lower the heat, and simmer, uncovered and stirring occasionally, until the liquid has evaporated and the mixture looks sticky and thick, about 60 minutes.

Remove the pan from the heat, and do a set test (page 10). If the marmalade isn't thick enough, return the pan to the heat for a few minutes, and then repeat the test.

Wash the jars, lids, and bands in very hot soapy water, rinse them well, and place them upside down on a clean towel to drain.

Spoon the marmalade into the jars, leaving a half inch of headroom to allow for expansion during freezing. Wipe the rims with a clean wet cloth or paper towel, add the lids and bands, and finger tighten the bands.

Label the jars. Cool completely and tighten the bands before storing the jars in the refrigerator or freezer.

QUICK IDEAS // Spread marmalade over a small wheel of brie set on a baking sheet, and bake at 400 degrees until the marmalade is bubbly and the cheese is oozy and soft. Try whisking a little mustard into the marmalade to glaze ham or smoked pork chops. Stir in chopped rosemary and parsley, and use it to stuff a pork loin or a pork chop.

orange cherry chutney

MAKES ABOUT 5 HALF-PINTS

Spicy-sweet and tangy, this chutney makes a fine condiment and a lovely gift. It's essential with curries, and you'll find yourself spooning it over soft cheese for a spread.

2 pounds organic navel oranges or other sweet oranges

2 cups water

1½ cups finely diced onion

1 cup dried tart cherries

1 cup rice vinegar

1 cup sugar

1 tablespoon minced garlic

1 tablespoon finely grated fresh ginger

1 tablespoon ground cumin

1 teaspoon crushed red pepper flakes

½ teaspoon salt

10 to 15 grinds black pepper

Scrub the oranges well under running water. Working with a vegetable peeler or a very sharp knife, remove wide strips of the zest from the fruit, being careful to avoid the white pith. (Save the oranges; you'll use them later in the recipe.) Examine the strips of zest, and use a sharp knife to scrape off any pith. Finely dice the zest.

In a small bowl, mix the zest and 1 cup of water. Cover the bowl, and allow the zest to macerate for at least 8 hours or overnight.

Drain the zest in a mesh strainer, and turn it into a 10-inch sauté pan.

With a sharp paring knife, remove the white pith from the oranges. Cut the oranges into small chunks, discarding any seeds. Add the oranges and 1 cup of water to the sauté pan along with the onion, cherries, vinegar, sugar, garlic, ginger, cumin, crushed red pepper flakes, salt, and pepper. Set the pan over medium heat, and bring the contents to a gentle boil. Lower the heat, and simmer, uncovered and stirring occasionally, until most of the liquid has evaporated and the chutney becomes glossy and thick, about 30 minutes. The chutney is done when you can drag a spoon across the bottom of the pan and the mixture holds its shape. Taste, and adjust the seasonings.

Wash the jars, lids, and bands in very hot soapy water, rinse them well, and place them upside down on a clean towel to drain.

Spoon the chutney into the jars, leaving a half inch of headroom to allow for expansion during freezing. Wipe the rims with a clean wet cloth or paper towel, add the lids and bands, and finger tighten the bands.

Label the jars. Cool completely and tighten the bands before storing the jars in the refrigerator or freezer.

QUICK IDEAS // Spread a layer of chutney on an open-face cheese sandwich or crackers; then run it under the broiler. Spoon the chutney over brie or chèvre to serve with crackers. Whisk the chutney into sour cream, and serve it as a dip with chips or vegetables.

sweet brined lemons

MAKES 2 TO 3 PINTS, DEPENDING ON THE SIZE OF THE LEMONS

These sweet-salty lemons are a simpler, easier version of Mette's traditional Danish recipe. We've simplified several of the steps to make the recipe easy and quick. Small lemons work the best. As with preserved limes, only the rind is used.

1 pound small organic lemons	2 teaspoons fennel seeds
¾ cup salt	1 teaspoon black peppercorns
3½ cups cider vinegar	2 dried árbol chilies or other hot peppers
1¼ cups packed light brown sugar	

Scrub the lemons well. Stand each lemon on end, and cut about three-quarters of the way through in two directions to create an X-shaped opening. Place the cut lemon on a plate, and stuff salt into the opening. Use a lot of salt. As you stuff the lemons with salt, place them in a single layer in a medium-size glass or stainless steel bowl. When you are done salting all the lemons, sprinkle the rest of the salt over them, along with any salt that has accumulated on the plate.

Cover the bowl with a plate and set it in the refrigerator for 2 weeks. Every day or so, turn the lemons over with a clean fork or spoon. A salt brine will start to form in the bowl.

After 2 weeks, combine the vinegar, brown sugar, fennel seeds, peppercorns, and chilies in a 10-inch sauté pan. Bring the liquid to a gentle boil over medium-high heat. Add the lemons, reduce the heat, and simmer, stirring gently, until the liquid is reduced and the lemons are very soft, about 20 to 30 minutes.

Wash the jars, lids, and bands in very hot soapy water, rinse them well, and place them upside down on a clean towel to drain.

Spoon the lemons into the jars along with the brine and spices. Cover each jar with a square of wax paper slightly larger than the jar opening, fold in the corners with a clean spoon, and push down gently so some of the brine comes up over the wax paper. Wipe the rims with a clean wet cloth or paper towel, add the lids and bands, and finger tighten the bands.

Label the jars. Cool completely and tighten the bands before storing the jars in the refrigerator.

QUICK IDEAS // Rinse and chop the lemon rind. Mix the chopped lemon rind with parsley to serve with fish or fish cakes. Toss it into a chickpea salad. Whisk it into mayonnaise for a sandwich spread or into yogurt for a dip.

candied citrus peel

MAKES ABOUT 4 HALF-PINTS

Freshly made candied peel is far tangier and much less sweet than the commercial product. For this recipe, we prefer fine sugar because it gives the resulting peel a delicate texture. To make Bonus! Citrus Syrup (page 124), be sure to save the peeled fruit and syrup.

2½ pounds organic citrus fruit (try a mix of grapefruit, lemons, and oranges)	1½ cups sugar
5 cups water	½ cup fine sugar (see note)

Working with a very sharp paring knife, follow the natural shape of the fruit to cut the peel in wide bands. Try to leave as much of the white pith on the fruit as possible. To remove any pith from the peel, lay the peel flat and scrape off the pith with the paring knife. Cut the peel into ¼-inch wide strips. Set the fruit aside.

In a medium pot, bring the water to a boil over high heat. Add the peel, lower the heat, and simmer until the peel is tender, about 15 minutes. Remove the peel with a slotted spoon, and set it aside. Reserve 2 cups of the cooking water.

In a medium saucepan, combine the reserved water and the 1½ cups of sugar. Bring the water to a boil over high heat, stirring to dissolve the sugar. Add the citrus peel to the syrup, lower the heat, and simmer for 10 minutes. Turn off the heat, and set the pan aside for 15 minutes.

Using a slotted spoon, transfer the peel to parchment-lined baking sheets, reserving the syrup to make Bonus! Citrus Syrup. Space the peel so it isn't touching, and let it dry until it is just tacky enough for the sugar to adhere, about 1 to 4 hours.

Turn the fine sugar into a medium bowl, add the peel, and toss to coat, using your fingers. Place the peel on baking sheets lined with fresh parchment to continue drying until it is no longer sticky, about 3 hours or overnight. Put the dried peel into clean, very dry jars. Store at room temperature.

NOTE: To make fine sugar, whiz sugar in a food processor, blender, or spice mill until the granules are very fine.

QUICK IDEAS // Chop the candied citrus peel, and fold it into cake, muffin, and cookie batters. Use it to garnish dessert plates of sweets or cheese.

bonus! citrus syrup

Tart and refreshing, this syrup is a real bonus! It will keep for months in the refrigerator and is great to have on hand.

reserved fruit from Candied Citrus Peel (page 123)
reserved syrup from Candied Citrus Peel

Cut the white pith from the fruit (it's OK to leave the seeds and membranes), and break the fruit into pieces. Place the fruit in a medium saucepan, and add the reserved syrup. Set the pan over medium heat, and bring the syrup a boil. Boil for 2 to 3 minutes, using a potato masher or a fork to further break up the fruit. Remove the pan from the heat, and let it cool for 15 minutes.

Place a medium mesh sieve over a deep bowl, and strain the fruit until no more liquid drips out. Refrain from pressing down on the fruit. Discard the solids left in the sieve.

Wash the jars, lids, and bands in very hot soapy water, rinse them well, and place them upside down on a clean towel to drain.

Spoon the syrup into the jars, leaving a half inch of headroom to allow for expansion during freezing. Wipe the rims with a clean wet cloth or paper towel, add the lids and bands, and finger tighten the bands.

Label the jars. Cool completely and tighten the bands before storing the jars in the refrigerator or freezer.

QUICK IDEAS // Whisk citrus syrup into a vinaigrette or marinade. Drizzle it over quick breads, muffins, cakes, and cupcakes when they are still warm from the oven. Beat the syrup into whipped cream or icing. Brush it on grilled pork chops, chicken, or lamb as a glaze.

cranberries

In the Nordic countries, lowbush cranberries (aka lingonberries) are a staple fruit. In the United States, Wisconsin's sandy marshes, home to sandhill cranes, are perfect for indigenous American cranberries. Loaded with vitamin C and high in antioxidants, all of these brilliant red berries (by any name) rank high among the world's most nutritious fruits.

rustic cranberry strawberry jam with lime and vanilla

MAKES ABOUT 4 HALF-PINTS

This delicious jam marries two opposite seasons. Make it in the summer with fresh strawberries and frozen cranberries, in fall with fresh cranberries and frozen strawberries, or with frozen fruit anytime of the year.

1 pound cranberries (about 4½ cups)	¾ cup sugar
10 ounces strawberries, cut into smaller pieces (about 2½ cups)	2 tablespoons lime juice
	2 tablespoons vanilla extract

Combine all the ingredients in a 10-inch sauté pan. Cover the pan, and macerate the fruit at room temperature for at least 2 hours or overnight.

Put a small plate in the freezer for the set test. Uncover the pan, and set it over medium heat, bring the contents to a gentle boil, and then lower the heat. Simmer, stirring occasionally and mashing the fruit with the back of a spoon or fork, until the mixture thickens, about 8 to 10 minutes.

Remove the pan from the heat, and do a set test (page 10). If the jam isn't thick enough, return the pan to the heat for a few minutes, and then repeat the test.

Wash the jars, lids, and bands in very hot soapy water, rinse them well, and place them upside down on a clean towel to drain.

Spoon the jam into the jars, leaving a half inch of headroom to allow for expansion during freezing. Wipe the rims with a clean wet cloth or paper towel, add the lids and bands, and finger tighten the bands.

Label the jars. Cool completely and tighten the bands before storing the jars in the refrigerator or freezer.

QUICK IDEAS // Slather this vibrant jam on thick slices of toasted pound cake, use it to fill layer cakes, beat it into icing for cookies and cupcakes. Whip it into cream to pile on gingerbread or lemon bars.

pickled cranberries

MAKES ABOUT 2 PINTS

Pickling amplifies the sweet-tart nature of the cranberry. The brine is so tasty that it doubles as a shrub, an old-fashioned fruit and vinegar drink.

1 pound cranberries (about 4½ cups)	¼ cup fresh red grapefruit juice
½ cup cider vinegar	4 wide bands red grapefruit zest
½ cup sugar	1 teaspoon ground fennel
¼ cup ruby port wine	

Wash the jars, lids, and bands in very hot soapy water, rinse them well, and place them upside down on a clean towel to drain.

Combine the cranberries, vinegar, and sugar in 10-inch sauté pan, and bring to a gentle boil over medium heat. Lower the heat, and simmer for just a few minutes. The cranberries should stay intact. Use a slotted spoon to transfer the cranberries to the jars, leaving the brine in the pan.

Add the port, grapefruit juice, zest, and fennel to the brine in the pan, and bring it back to a gentle boil for a few minutes to blend the flavors.

Place 2 pieces of grapefruit zest in each jar, and add the brine, leaving a half inch of headroom to allow for expansion during freezing. Cover each jar with a square of wax paper slightly larger than the jar opening, fold in the corners with a clean spoon, and push down gently so some of the brine comes up over the wax paper. Wipe the rims with a clean wet cloth or paper towel, add the lids and bands, and finger tighten the bands.

Label the jars. Cool completely and tighten the bands before storing the jars in the refrigerator or freezer. Let the cranberries rest for a couple of weeks in the refrigerator to allow the flavors to marry.

QUICK IDEAS // Beautiful on a cheese board and alongside a rich pâté, pickled cranberries are also wonderful tossed into a wild rice salad. Try mixing a little sparkling water or Prosecco with the brine for a refreshing drink. Add a shot of vodka or rum to the brine, and you have an elegant cocktail.

cranberry ketchup

It's only in recent years that *ketchup* has meant a tomato sauce. Here, tangy cranberries spiced with cinnamon, cloves, allspice, and peppercorns make a fragrant, intense sauce.

1 pound cranberries (about 4½ cups)	1½ teaspoons yellow mustard seeds
1 cup water	½ cup sugar
1 cup medium-diced red onions	½ cup rice vinegar
½ teaspoon whole cloves	1-inch piece ginger, peeled and thinly sliced
1 teaspoon whole allspice	½ cinnamon stick
1 teaspoon black peppercorns	1 teaspoon salt
1½ teaspoons celery seeds	

Combine the cranberries, water, and onions in a 10-inch sauté pan and bring to a gentle boil over medium heat. Reduce the heat, and simmer, uncovered and stirring occasionally, until the onions are soft and the cranberries have popped, about 15 to 20 minutes. If the mixture starts to look too dry, add up to another ½ cup of water.

Place a medium mesh sieve over a deep bowl. Working in batches, press the cranberry mixture through the sieve, scraping the underside of the sieve with a clean spoon. Discard the solids left in the sieve, and clean the sieve.

Turn the cranberry puree and the cloves, allspice, peppercorns, celery seed, mustard seed, sugar, vinegar, ginger, cinnamon, and salt into a 10-inch sauté pan. Measure the depth of the puree in the pan using the dipstick method (page 9).

Set the pan over medium-high heat, bring the puree to a gentle boil, and lower the heat. Simmer, uncovered, stirring occasionally, until the mixture has thickened and reduced by a third to a half, about 30 minutes. The ketchup will thicken a bit more as it cools.

Place the cleaned medium mesh sieve over a deep bowl or pot, and work the ketchup through the sieve. Discard the spices.

Wash the jars, lids, and bands in very hot soapy water, rinse them well, and place them upside down on a clean towel to drain.

Spoon the ketchup into the jars, leaving a half inch of headroom to allow for expansion during freezing. Wipe the rims with a clean wet cloth or paper towel, add the lids and bands, and finger tighten the bands.

Label the jars. Cool completely and tighten the bands before storing the jars in the refrigerator or freezer.

QUICK IDEAS // Use this lush, thick spread as you would any ketchup—on burgers and fries. It's especially good with oven-fried sweet potatoes, grilled turkey burgers, and turkey sausages.

currants

Old-fashioned currants are making a comeback. These perennial bushes perform beautifully in our cool climate and produce intense, tart, gem-like fruit. Fresh currants do not ship or store especially well, so you won't find them in most supermarkets. But currants are super easy to grow yourself in a cool northern climate, and you can also find them at the farmers market.

black currant preserves with rum

MAKES ABOUT 5 HALF-PINTS

Black currants have a strong, tart flavor. Once cooked, they mellow to become a beautiful jam, preserve, or shrub (old-fashioned fruit and vinegar drink). The leaves have subtle black currant flavor and, when finely minced, can be added to fruit butters and compotes. The fruit is extremely high in antioxidants, vitamin C, and iron. This preserve is rich, dark, and slightly decadent. You'll want to eat it right out of the jar as soon as it's cooled.

2 pounds black currants (7 to 8 cups)	½ cup rum
1½ cups sugar	1 teaspoon finely grated lime zest
½ cup water	

Put a small plate in the freezer for the set test. Combine all of the ingredients in a 10-inch sauté pan. Bring it to a gentle boil over medium heat; then lower the heat. Simmer, uncovered, stirring occasionally, until the mixture thickens, about 15 minutes. Remove the pan from the heat, and do a set test (page 10). If the preserves aren't firm enough, return the pan to the heat for a few minutes, and then repeat the test.

Wash the jars, lids, and bands in very hot soapy water, rinse them well, and place them upside down on a clean towel to drain.

Spoon the preserves into the jars, leaving a half inch of headroom to allow for expansion during freezing. Wipe the rims with a clean wet cloth or paper towel, add the lids and bands, and finger tighten the bands.

Label the jars. Cool completely and tighten the bands before storing the jars in the refrigerator or freezer.

QUICK IDEAS // Whisk together equal parts whipped cream and preserves, put it in the freezer until slightly firm, and serve it in parfait glasses for dessert. Fill tarts, pies, cakes, and thumbprint cookies with the preserves. Spoon the preserves into a meringue shell, and top it with cream and berries.

black currant jam with candied ginger and lemon thyme

MAKES ABOUT 3 HALF-PINTS

This jam is deep and smoky with the true taste of the black currants. For a more subtle flavor, include white and red currants in the mix. Lemon thyme has a less assertive flavor than other varieties of thyme. If it isn't available, use less thyme and add a grating of lemon zest.

1½ pounds black currants (5 to 6 cups)

¾ cup sugar

¼ cup slivered Candied Ginger (page 171)

¼ cup water

4 sprigs lemon thyme

Put a small plate in the freezer for the set test. Combine all of the ingredients in a 10-inch sauté pan. Bring to a gentle simmer over medium heat; then lower the heat so that small bubbles are barely bursting on the surface. Cook uncovered, stirring occasionally, until the jam thickens, about 15 minutes. Remove the pan from the heat, and do a set test (page 10). If the jam isn't thick enough, return the pan to the heat for a few minutes, and then repeat the test. Remove and discard the lemon thyme.

Wash the jars, lids, and bands in very hot soapy water, rinse them well, and place them upside down on a clean towel to drain.

Spoon the jam into the jars, leaving a half inch of headroom to allow for expansion during freezing. Wipe the rims with a clean wet cloth or paper towel, add the lids and bands, and finger tighten the bands.

Label the jars. Cool completely and tighten the bands before storing the jars in the refrigerator or freezer.

QUICK IDEAS // Spoon this lush jam over vanilla ice cream. Use it to top shortbread, and add a dollop of whipped cream. It's great in yogurt!

lavender-scented white currant syrup

MAKES ABOUT 3 HALF-PINTS

White currants are the sweetest of the currants, almost translucent little jewels that the birds ignore because they can't see them. We've added a little lemon juice to enhance the citrusy notes, a perfect match for lavender in this refreshing syrup.

3 pounds white currants (about 10 cups)	2 tablespoons culinary dried lavender
1 cup water	2 wide bands lemon zest
1 cup sugar	

Combine the white currants and water in a 10-inch sauté pan. Bring the water to a boil over medium-high heat. Lower the heat, mash the fruit to release the juice, and simmer, uncovered, until the fruit is very soft, about 10 to 15 minutes.

Place a colander lined with a clean towel or cheesecloth over a deep bowl. Pour in the fruit mixture, and let it strain for at least 2 hours or overnight. Gather the corners of the cloth and squeeze to extract the juice, scraping the underside of the cloth with a spoon. Discard the fruit pulp left in the cloth. Measure the juice: you should have about 2½ cups.

Pour the strained juice back into the sauté pan, and add the sugar, lavender, and lemon zest. Bring the syrup to a gentle boil over medium heat. Lower the heat, and simmer, uncovered and stirring occasionally, just until the sugar is dissolved, about 6 to 8 minutes. Cooked too long, syrup becomes jelly.

Wash the jars, lids, and bands in very hot soapy water, rinse them well, and place them upside down on a clean towel to drain.

Pour the syrup into the jars, leaving a half inch of headroom to allow for expansion during freezing. Wipe the rims with a clean wet cloth or paper towel, add the lids and bands, and finger tighten the bands.

Label the jars. Cool completely and tighten the bands before storing the jars in the refrigerator or freezer.

QUICK IDEAS // This syrup makes a fabulous cocktail when cut with sparkling water and a shot of gin, vodka, or rum. Stir it into iced tea, drizzle it over ice cream, or whip it into cream cheese for a heady spread.

sweet and hot red currant relish

Gorgeous ruby-colored currants are as good in savory dishes as they are in sweets. This lively condiment is vibrant, spicy, and tangy. Keep some for yourself, and give the rest as gifts.

3	tablespoons olive oil	1½	cups white balsamic vinegar
2	cups finely diced red onion	1	cup sugar
1¼	cups finely diced sweet red pepper	3	star anise
¼	cup finely diced Fresno, red jalapeño, or other medium-hot red pepper	2	teaspoons ground allspice
		2	teaspoons English hot mustard powder
¼	cup minced garlic	2	teaspoons salt
2	tablespoons finely grated fresh ginger	1	pound red currants (about 4 cups)

Place the oil, onion, and sweet red pepper in a 10-inch sauté pan set over medium-low heat. Sauté the vegetables until they are soft but not browned, about 8 to 10 minutes. Scrape the vegetables into a bowl, and set it aside.

Put the hot pepper, garlic, ginger, and ¾ cup of the vinegar in the pan, and bring it to a boil. Cook until most of the vinegar has evaporated, about 5 to 8 minutes. Stir in the sautéed vegetables, the remaining ¾ cup of vinegar, and the sugar, star anise, allspice, mustard, and salt. Taste, and adjust the seasoning.

Set the pan over medium-high heat, bring to a gentle boil, and cook until the liquid begins to thicken, about 15 to 20 minutes. Carefully fold the currants into the mixture. Continue cooking until the currants are near bursting but still intact, another 5 minutes. The mixture should be glossy and loosely hold its shape. Remove and discard the star anise.

Wash the jars, lids, and bands in very hot soapy water, rinse them well, and place them upside down on a clean towel to drain.

Spoon the relish into the jars, leaving a half inch of headroom to allow for expansion during freezing. Wipe the rims with a clean wet cloth or paper towel, add the lids and bands, and finger tighten the bands.

Label the jars. Cool completely and tighten the bands before storing the jars in the refrigerator or freezer.

QUICK IDEAS // This relish is fabulous with roast turkey and on turkey burgers and brats. Serve it over young, fresh cheeses, and whisk it into mayonnaise for a sandwich spread or dip.

dried fruit

Dried fruit plays a big role in Nordic cuisine, especially in special soups served during the holidays. Drying concentrates the fruit's natural flavor, so you get a sweet conserve without having to add much sugar.

QUICK TIP // Use a sharp kitchen shears to cut dried fruit; too often it sticks to the knife blade.

boozy fruits

MAKES ABOUT 3 HALF-PINTS

When dried fruit is soaked in spirits, it becomes plump and tender, ready for prime-time desserts. For a kid-friendly version, use a good-quality unsweetened apple or white grape juice.

1¼ cups dry sherry

1 teaspoon cardamom pods, lightly crushed

4 ounces dried blueberries (about ¾ cup)

4 ounces dried tart cherries (about ¾ cup)

4 ounces apple juice–sweetened dried cranberries (about ¾ cup)

Combine the sherry and cardamom pods in a small saucepan set over medium-high heat, and bring the sherry to a gentle boil. Turn off the heat, cover the pan, and let it sit to infuse for 10 minutes.

Place the dried fruit in a medium bowl. Strain the sherry into the fruit, and discard the cardamom pods. Mix well and cover. Let the bowl sit at room temperature until the fruit has rehydrated and is plump, about 2 hours.

Wash the jars, lids, and bands in very hot soapy water, rinse them well, and place them upside down on a clean towel to drain.

Divide the fruit and sherry among the jars. Cover each jar with a square of wax paper slightly larger than the jar opening, fold in the corners with a clean spoon, and push down gently so some of the sherry comes up over the wax paper. Wipe the rims with a clean wet cloth or paper towel, add the lids, and tighten the bands.

Label the jars, and store them in the refrigerator.

QUICK IDEAS // Toss Boozy Fruit into fruit salad; spoon it over crème brûlée or vanilla ice cream. Add a little cumin and coriander, and serve it with grilled lamb.

apricot prune jam

MAKES 4 TO 5 HALF-PINTS

There is nothing simpler than making jam with dried fruit. You soak the fruit overnight, do a little prep the next day, and then cook it for 5 minutes! Try different fruit juices, such as apple and pear, to vary the flavors in this easy recipe.

½ pound dried apricots, coarsely chopped (about 1½ cups)

½ pound prunes, coarsely chopped (about 1½ cups)

2 cups unsweetened white grape juice

½ cup fresh red grapefruit juice

3 tablespoons fresh lime juice

1 tablespoon finely grated lime zest

½ teaspoon ground cardamom

Combine the apricots, prunes, and grape juice in a 10-inch sauté pan. Cover the pan, and let the fruit rehydrate at room temperature for at least 8 hours or overnight.

Transfer the fruit to a food processor fitted with a steel blade, and pulse a few times to roughly chop it. Be careful not to puree the fruit.

Pour the fruit mixture back into the sauté pan, and add the grapefruit juice, lime juice, zest, and cardamom. Bring it to a gentle boil over medium heat; then lower the heat. Simmer, uncovered, stirring occasionally, to combine the flavors, about 5 minutes. If the jam appears dry, add a few tablespoons of water.

Wash the jars, lids, and bands in very hot soapy water, rinse them well, and place them upside down on a clean towel to drain.

Spoon the jam into the jars, leaving a half inch of headroom to allow for expansion during freezing. Wipe the rims with a clean wet cloth or paper towel, add the lids and bands, and finger tighten the bands.

Label the jars. Cool completely and tighten the bands before storing the jars in the refrigerator or freezer.

QUICK IDEAS // Serve the jam on hot oatmeal and top it with a sprinkle of chopped hazelnuts. Whip the jam into cream cheese; roll it into a strudel. Stir a little into pound cake batter.

elderberries

Elderberries, loaded with antioxidants, are the basis for traditional cordials and cold-fighting elixirs in Nordic households. They grow abundantly in our northern climates, and we're beginning to see small producers market them through co-ops and farmers markets. Don't eat them raw, when they can be very tannic: they come into their own when cooked.

Elderberries are messy. The juice stains clothes, hands, and porous surfaces. Years ago, they were the key ingredient in purple dye. The easiest way to remove the berries from their stalks is to strip them using the tines of a fork.

elderberry and lemon thyme shrub

MAKES 2 TO 3 HALF-PINTS

Loaded with vitamin C and antioxidants, this old-fashioned shrub is not just good for you; it's delicious too!

⅔ pound cleaned elderberries (about 2 cups)

1 cup water

¾ cup sugar

3 large sprigs lemon thyme

1 cup cider vinegar

In a 10-inch sauté pan, combine the elderberries, water, sugar, and lemon thyme. Bring it to a gentle boil over medium-high heat; then reduce the heat. Simmer, uncovered, occasionally mashing the fruit with a fork, until the berries are soft and have released their juices, about 15 minutes.

Place a fine mesh sieve over a deep bowl, pour in the fruit mixture, and press it with the back of a spoon to extract the juice. You should have about 1⅔ cups. Cool the juice before stirring in the vinegar.

Wash the jars, lids, and bands in very hot soapy water, rinse them well, and place them upside down on a clean towel to drain.

Pour the shrub into the jars, leaving a half inch of headroom to allow for expansion during freezing. Wipe the rims with a clean wet cloth or paper towel, add the lids and bands, and finger tighten the bands.

Label the jars. Cool completely and tighten the bands before storing the jars in the refrigerator or freezer.

QUICK IDEAS // Cut this tangy shrub with ginger ale, sparkling water, or champagne. Cheers!

elderberry apple butter

A cross between a fruit butter and a soft jam, this pretty, tart spread makes a wonderful gift. It's rich and satisfying, not too sweet. No need to peel or core the apples; in fact, the skin and seeds add pectin to help set this smooth, spicy fruit butter. The thickness is determined by the tartness—and hence the pectin level—of the apples. The tarter the apples, the thicker the fruit butter.

1½ cups water	3 cups cleaned elderberries
3 tablespoons lemon juice	(about 1 pound)
4 cups coarsely chopped apples	1 cup sugar
(about 1¼ pounds)	2 teaspoons ground ginger

In a 10-inch sauté pan, combine the water, 1 tablespoon of the lemon juice, and the apples. Over medium-high heat, bring the water to a gentle boil. Lower the heat, and simmer, uncovered and stirring occasionally, until the apples are tender, about 10 minutes. Add the elderberries and simmer, stirring, until tender, about 10 minutes more.

Turn the mixture into a medium mesh sieve, and use a wooden spoon to push and press the fruit through. Discard the fruit left in the sieve.

Measure the cooked fruit as you return it to the sauté pan. You should have about 4 cups. If not, adjust the amount of sugar, lemon juice, and ginger accordingly.

Stir in the sugar, the remaining 2 tablespoons of lemon juice, and the ginger. Bring the fruit butter to a gentle boil over medium-high heat, and then lower the heat. Simmer, uncovered and stirring occasionally, until the sugar dissolves, about 5 minutes.

Wash the jars, lids, and bands in very hot soapy water, rinse them well, and place them upside down on a clean towel to drain.

Spoon the fruit butter into the jars, leaving a half inch of headroom to allow for expansion during freezing. Wipe the rims with a clean wet cloth or paper towel, add the lids and bands, and finger tighten the bands.

Label the jars. Cool completely and tighten the bands before storing the jars in the refrigerator or freezer.

QUICK IDEAS // Layer the fruit butter into cakes, spoon it into yogurt, and use it to fill tarts and pies. Roll it into a crepe, and sandwich it between ginger cookies.

gooseberries

The gooseberry is a funny berry, resembling a hairy green or red grape. It's too tart to eat raw, even when ripe. But we'd argue that these hardy perennial fruits deserve a little love. They make terrific savory chutneys and lovely jam. Gooseberries are indigenous to the Nordic countries and came to North America with early settlers. Find them at farmers markets and co-ops.

gooseberry jam with lemon and vanilla

MAKES ABOUT 4 HALF-PINTS

Vanilla amps up the muscat grape flavor of gooseberries. The jam freezes beautifully and is good enough to eat with a spoon.

2 pounds gooseberries (about 7 cups)	2 tablespoons fresh lemon juice
1 cup sugar	1 teaspoon finely grated lemon zest
½ cup water	1 vanilla bean, split in half lengthwise

Put a small plate in the freezer for the set test. With a sharp paring knife, cut off the blossom and stem ends of the gooseberries. Rinse the gooseberries well.

Combine the gooseberries, sugar, water, lemon juice, zest, and vanilla bean in a 10-inch sauté pan. Bring the mixture to a gentle boil over medium-high heat; then lower the heat. Simmer, uncovered and stirring occasionally, until the mixture has thickened, about 30 minutes. Discard the vanilla bean.

Remove the pan from the heat, and do a set test (page 10). If the jam isn't thick enough, return the pan to the heat for a few minutes, and then repeat the test.

Wash the jars, lids, and bands in very hot soapy water, rinse them well, and place them upside down on a clean towel to drain.

Spoon the jam into the jars, leaving a half inch of headroom to allow for expansion during freezing. Wipe the rims with a clean wet cloth or paper towel, add the lids and bands, and finger tighten the bands.

Label the jars. Cool completely and tighten the bands before storing the jars in the refrigerator or freezer.

QUICK IDEAS // Fold this jam into whipped cream, slather it on layers of sponge cake or lady fingers, and then drizzle on some sherry for a spirited dessert. Of course, this jam is made for rich, buttery scones served with tea.

gooseberry chutney

Gooseberries are tangy enough for savory dishes, and when sweetened, their assertive nature is tamed to a subtle raisin-like taste. This recipe makes the most of both qualities. We prefer red gooseberries, which tend to be a little sweeter, in this recipe.

2 tablespoons sunflower oil	¾ cup sugar
¼ cup finely diced red onion	1 cup rice vinegar
1 pound gooseberries (about 3½ cups)	1 teaspoon crushed red pepper flakes

Put the oil and onions into a 10-inch sauté pan set over medium-high heat, and cook until the onions are soft and translucent, about 7 to 10 minutes. Be careful not to brown the onions. Add the gooseberries, sugar, vinegar, and crushed red pepper flakes, bring to a gentle boil, and then lower the heat. Simmer, uncovered, stirring occasionally, until the mixture is quite thick, about 40 to 45 minutes. The chutney is done when you can drag a large spoon across the bottom of the pan and the mixture holds its shape.

Wash the jars, lids, and bands in very hot soapy water, rinse them well, and place them upside down on a clean towel to drain.

Spoon the chutney into the jars, leaving a half inch of headroom to allow for expansion during freezing. Wipe the rims with a clean wet cloth or paper towel, add the lids and bands, and finger tighten the bands.

Label the jars. Cool completely and tighten the bands before storing the jars in the refrigerator or freezer.

QUICK IDEAS // This chutney is especially good with chicken or vegetable curry and as a garnish to curried pumpkin or squash soup. It's great with cheddar cheese, rich pork pâtés, and smoked salmon.

grapes

You can use your backyard grapes or any supermarket grapes in this recipe, and you don't need to seed them. The University of Minnesota's cold-hardy grapes have launched the state's wine industry and provide backyard gardeners and cooks with fresh fruit in season.

spicy grape bbq sauce

MAKES ABOUT 4 HALF-PINTS

This is one of the easiest and tastiest ways to put up backyard grapes; any table grape will work nicely as well.

4 pounds grapes, stemmed and washed (about 12 cups)	1 teaspoon ground chipotle pepper
1 cup water	2 teaspoons ground allspice
1½ cups sugar	2 teaspoons English mustard powder
¾ cup red wine vinegar	1 teaspoon cayenne pepper
¼ cup balsamic vinegar	1 teaspoon ground ginger

Put the grapes and water into a heavy-bottomed pot. Bring it to a boil over medium-high heat; then reduce the heat. Simmer, covered, for 15 to 20 minutes, occasionally mashing the grapes to release the juices.

Place a medium mesh sieve over a deep bowl. Working in batches, press the grape mash through the sieve, scraping the underside of the sieve with a clean spoon. Discard the solids left in the sieve. You should have about 5 cups of juice. If not, add a little water.

Transfer the juice into a 10-inch sauté pan, and add the sugar, vinegars, chipotle, allspice, mustard, cayenne, and ginger. Measure the depth of the liquid using the dipstick method (page 9). Set the pan over medium-high heat, bring the sauce to a boil, and then reduce the heat. Simmer, uncovered, until the sauce has reduced by half, stirring occasionally and skimming any foam from the surface, about 30 minutes.

Wash the jars, lids, and bands in very hot soapy water, rinse them well, and place them upside down on a clean towel to drain.

Pour the BBQ sauce into the jars, leaving a half inch of headroom to allow for expansion during freezing. Wipe the rims with a clean wet cloth or paper towel, add the lids and bands, and finger tighten the bands.

Label the jars. Cool completely and tighten the bands before storing the jars in the refrigerator or freezer.

QUICK IDEAS // Spicy-sweet, this sauce makes a terrific dip for fries and chips. Slather it over a grilled pork chop or chicken breast. Brush it over grilled or roasted carrots.

pears

Pick a local pear—preferably a Luscious Pear! The name says it all. These tiny pears are slightly mellow, fragrant, and tender. Don't be put off by their mottled, rough yellow skins; they are far better tasting than they look. If you're pressed for time, simply make pear butter, following the recipe for Applesauce with Grapefruit and Cardamom (page 97) or Caramel Apple Butter with Lemongrass (page 98).

NOTE: Like apples, sliced pears tend to brown quickly, so keep them in acidified water until you're ready to use them.

lime ginger pear shrub

MAKES ABOUT 7 HALF-PINTS

This recipe dates back to pioneer times, when vinegar syrups were the base for any number of refreshing drinks served out in the hot fields. Cut this shrub with sparkling water and garnish it with a slice of lime; add a splash of vodka or rum, and you have a winning cocktail.

⅔ cup loosely packed coarsely
　grated ginger
2 tablespoons lime juice
1 cup sugar

3 pounds very ripe pears, coarsely
　chopped (about 7 to 8 cups)
1 cup cider vinegar

Combine the ginger, lime juice, and sugar in a medium bowl. Add the pears as you cut them. Crush the pears with a potato masher or a fork to release their juice.

Tightly cover the bowl with plastic wrap, and set the bowl on the countertop out of direct sunlight. Macerate the fruit for at least 8 hours or overnight.

Place a medium mesh sieve over a large bowl. Working in batches, press the pear mixture through the sieve, scraping the underside of the sieve with a clean spoon. Discard the solids left in the sieve. Stir in the vinegar.

Wash the jars, lids, and bands in very hot soapy water, rinse them well, and place them upside down on a clean towel to drain.

Pour the shrub into the jars, leaving a half inch of headroom to allow for expansion during freezing. Wipe the rims with a clean wet cloth or paper towel, add the lids and bands, and tighten the bands.

Label the jars, and store them in the refrigerator or freezer.

QUICK IDEAS // This old-timey concoction is surprisingly refreshing on a hot summer's day. Mix ¼ cup of shrub into 1 cup of sparkling or still water, and serve over ice. Add a jigger of rum or vodka for a very elegant cocktail.

sweet and spicy pear chutney

MAKES ABOUT 5 HALF-PINTS

Subtly spiced with Aleppo peppers, a mainstay in the Middle East, this easy chutney makes a great last-minute gift.

CHUTNEY

- 2 tablespoons sunflower oil
- 1 cup medium-diced red onion
- 2 tablespoons minced garlic
- 2 tablespoons finely grated fresh ginger
- 1 teaspoon crushed red pepper flakes
- 1 tablespoon Aleppo pepper or ancho pepper
- 3 pounds ripe pears, peeled, cored, and medium-diced (about 6 cups), held in acidified water (page 95)
- 1 cup water

- ½ cup rice vinegar
- ½ cup sugar
- 1 teaspoon salt

SPICE BAG

- 1 tablespoon yellow mustard seeds
- 3 bay leaves
- 2 teaspoons whole allspice
- 2 teaspoons cardamom seeds
- 2 teaspoons coriander seeds
- ¼ teaspoon whole cloves

Put the oil, onion, garlic, ginger, crushed red pepper flakes, and Aleppo pepper in a 10-inch sauté pan set over medium-high heat. Cook, stirring, until the onions are translucent and the mixture is very fragrant, about 5 to 7 minutes. Be careful not to brown the onions.

Drain the pears, and add them to the pan along with the water, vinegar, sugar, and salt. Place the mustard seeds, bay leaves, allspice, cardamom, coriander, and cloves in a spice bag or square of cheesecloth, and place it in the pan. Increase the heat to bring the mixture to a boil; then reduce the heat. Simmer, uncovered, and stir until most of the liquid has evaporated and the mixture looks sticky and gooey, about 30 to 40 minutes. The timing will depend on the ripeness of the pears. The chutney is done when you can drag a large spoon across the bottom of the pan and the mixture holds its shape. Remove the spice bag.

Wash the jars, lids, and bands in very hot soapy water, rinse them well, and place them upside down on a clean towel to drain.

Spoon the chutney into the jars, leaving a half inch of headroom to allow for expansion during freezing. Wipe the rims with a clean wet cloth or paper towel, add the lids and bands, and finger tighten the bands.

Label the jars. Cool completely and tighten the bands before storing the jars in the refrigerator or freezer.

QUICK IDEAS // Layer the chutney into a grilled cheese sandwich. Spoon it over cream cheese to serve with crackers. Whisk the chutney into mayonnaise for a salad or sandwich spread.

sweet and savory pickled pears

MAKES ABOUT 3 TO 4 PINTS

Tart and crisp, these pickled pears are more versatile than pears in syrup, venturing where sweeter pears dare not tread. Choose firm, slightly underripe pears for this recipe.

2 cups water

¾ cup cider vinegar

½ cup honey

½ cup sugar

1½-inch piece ginger, peeled and thinly sliced

3 to 4 bay leaves

3 pounds underripe pears, peeled, cored, and cut into wedges, held in acidified water (page 95)

1 teaspoon black peppercorns, slightly crushed

Combine the water, vinegar, honey, sugar, ginger, and bay leaves in a 10-inch sauté pan set over medium-high heat. Bring to a gentle boil, stirring to dissolve the sugar. Add the pears, reduce the heat, and simmer, uncovered, skimming any foam from the surface, until the pears are tender but still firm, about 5 minutes.

Wash the jars, lids, and bands in very hot soapy water, rinse them well, and place them upside down on a clean towel to drain.

Using a slotted spoon, remove the pears from the liquid and place them in the jars. Divide the spices among the jars, and pour in the hot brine, leaving a half inch of head-room. Cover each jar with a square of wax paper slightly larger than the jar opening, fold in the corners with a clean spoon, and push down gently so some of the brine comes up over the wax paper. Wipe the rims with a clean wet cloth or paper towel, add the lids and bands, and finger tighten the bands.

Label the jars. Cool completely and tighten the bands before storing the jars in the refrigerator. Let the pears rest for a couple of weeks in the refrigerator to allow the flavors to marry.

QUICK IDEAS // These pears are just sweet enough to garnish a cheesecake or a dense pound cake. Toss chopped pears into a green salad with spiced nuts. They're great served alongside grilled or roast pork. Use any leftover brine in a vinaigrette or a cocktail.

plums

There are a few tricks for working with plums. Make sure they're very ripe so the sugars and juices are at their peak. To remove the pits of the clingstone varieties, slice down one side of the plum parallel to the natural seam in the fruit, a little off center. This matches the direction of the pit. Cut off both sides and trim around the pit with the tip of your knife to remove any excess fruit. Then you're good to go.

chunky plum compote

If you can't find ground fennel seeds, grind your own in a spice mill or coffee grinder. Alternatively, place them in a resealable plastic bag, and crush them with a heavy object, such as a rolling pin or a pot. Their coarse texture adds a nice crunch to the compote.

⅓ cup sugar

¾ cup finely diced shallots

1 star anise

1 teaspoon ground fennel

1 teaspoon ground coriander

1 teaspoon crushed red pepper flakes

1 teaspoon salt

1½ pounds plums, pitted and coarsely chopped (about 4 cups)

3 tablespoons white balsamic vinegar

10 to 15 grinds black pepper

Pour the sugar into a 10-inch sauté pan, and slowly cook the sugar over low heat until it melts and turns a pale brown. Stir in the shallots, star anise, fennel, coriander, crushed red pepper flakes, and salt. Increase the heat a little, continue stirring to prevent sticking, and cook until the shallots are soft and translucent, about 10 minutes. Stir in the plums, vinegar, and freshly ground pepper. If the mixture starts to look dry, add a little water. Simmer the compote, stirring occasionally, until it starts to thicken and most of the liquid has evaporated, about 10 minutes.

Wash the jars, lids, and bands in very hot soapy water, rinse them well, and place them upside down on a clean towel to drain.

Spoon the compote into the jars, leaving a half inch of headroom to allow for expansion during freezing. Wipe the rims with a clean wet cloth or paper towel, add the lids and bands, and finger tighten the bands.

Label the jars. Cool completely and tighten the bands before storing the jars in the refrigerator or freezer.

QUICK IDEAS // Pair this beautiful compote with tangy chèvre, creamy fresh ricotta, or an assertive cheddar or blue cheese.

roasted plum chutney

MAKES 3 TO 4 HALF-PINTS

Cooking the chutney in the oven helps keep the plum pieces intact. It's easiest to use prune plums or elongated bluish-purple freestone plums that are easy to pit. Do not use an aluminum baking dish: it will react with the vinegar, resulting in a chutney that is off-color and off-flavor.

CHUTNEY

- 2 pounds prune plums, pitted and quartered
- ½ cup sugar
- ½ cup rice vinegar
- ½ teaspoon ground chipotle pepper

SPICE BAG

- ½ teaspoon black peppercorns
- 2 bay leaves
- 1 teaspoon coriander seeds
- 1 teaspoon whole cardamom pods, slightly crushed

Preheat the oven to 325 degrees. Place the plums in a baking dish that is large enough to allow for a single layer. Add the sugar and vinegar, and stir well. Sprinkle the chipotle over the plums. Fill a spice bag or a square of cheesecloth with the peppercorns, bay leaves, coriander, and cardamom. Nestle the spice bag in among the plums.

Place the uncovered baking dish on the oven's middle rack. Stir gently every 15 minutes until the liquid becomes thick and syrupy and the plums are soft but still hold their shape, about 30 to 45 minutes, depending on the size of the plum pieces. The chutney is done when you can drag a large spoon across the bottom of the pan and the mixture holds its shape. The syrup will continue to thicken as it cools. After the chutney is cooked, remove and discard the spice bag.

Wash the jars, lids, and bands in very hot soapy water, rinse them well, and place them upside down on a clean towel to drain.

Spoon the chutney into the jars, leaving a half inch of headroom to allow for expansion during freezing. Wipe the rims with a clean wet cloth or paper towel, add the lids and bands, and finger tighten the bands.

Label the jars. Cool completely and tighten the bands before storing the jars in the refrigerator or freezer.

QUICK IDEAS // A natural partner to pork—grilled, roasted, sautéed—this lush, smooth chutney is also great with hard cheeses and preserved meats.

plum jam with port wine

MAKES ABOUT 2 HALF-PINTS

This recipe is simple to make, yet complexly flavored thanks to the port wine. Choose a good ruby port with nice body.

⅔ pound ripe plums, pitted and coarsely
    chopped (about 2 cups)
½ cup ruby port wine
½ cup sugar

Put a small plate in the freezer for the set test. Combine the plums, port, and sugar in a 10-inch sauté pan. Cover the pan, and macerate the fruit at room temperature for 30 to 60 minutes.

Uncover the pan, set it over medium heat, and bring it to a gentle boil. Lower the heat and simmer, stirring occasionally, until the plums are very soft, about 20 minutes.

Remove the pan from the heat, and do a set test (page 10). If the jam isn't thick enough, return the pan to the heat for a few minutes, and then repeat the test.

Wash the jars, lids, and bands in very hot soapy water, rinse them well, and place them upside down on a clean towel to drain.

Spoon the jam into the jars, leaving a half inch of headroom to allow for expansion during freezing. Wipe the rims with a clean wet cloth or paper towel, add the lids and bands, and finger tighten the bands.

Label the jars. Cool completely and tighten the bands before storing the jars in the refrigerator or freezer.

QUICK IDEAS // This elegant jam makes a wonderful filling for a tart, a topping for vanilla ice cream, and a fine spread for buttery toast.

raspberries

Raspberries are the taste of summer. Thanks to the everbearing varieties, we get crops of fruit at the beginning and the end of the growing season. Wild raspberries are tinier and seedier than the cultivated fruit, but they are intensely flavored and add extra punch to any jam.

minty raspberry jam

MAKES ABOUT 4 HALF-PINTS

This brightly colored, bold jam says summer all year long. Try using different varieties of mint. Chocolate, orange, pineapple—these mints all add their subtle notes.

2 pounds raspberries (about 8 cups)	1½ tablespoons fresh lemon juice
1½ cups sugar	1 tablespoon finely grated lemon zest
2 tablespoons minced fresh mint	

Place the raspberries in a 10-inch sauté pan, sprinkle the sugar, mint, lemon juice, and zest over the berries, and gently stir everything together with a large spoon. Cover the pan, and macerate the fruit at room temperature for at least 2 hours or overnight. The sugar will draw the juices from the raspberries, yet they'll remain intact.

Put a small plate in the freezer for the set test. Uncover the pan, set it over medium heat, and bring it to a gentle boil. Reduce the heat and simmer, stirring carefully, until the mixture has thickened, about 10 to 12 minutes.

Remove the pan from the heat, and do a set test (page 10). If the jam isn't thick enough, return the pan to the heat for a few minutes, and then repeat the test.

Wash the jars, lids, and bands in very hot soapy water, rinse them well, and place them upside down on a clean towel to drain.

Spoon the jam into the jars, leaving a half inch of headroom to allow for expansion during freezing. Wipe the rims with a clean wet cloth or paper towel, add the lids and bands, and finger tighten the bands.

Label the jars. Cool completely and tighten the bands before storing the jars in the refrigerator or freezer.

QUICK IDEAS // Use this jam to top a cheesecake or fill muffins and cupcakes. Whisk the jam into frostings and whipped cream.

chipotle raspberry syrup

MAKES 3 TO 5 HALF-PINTS

This recipe calls for an extraordinary amount of raspberries, just the thing for bountiful backyard raspberry canes and overly optimistic pick-your-own farm outings. The idea for this syrup may seem indulgent, but the flavor is memorable: slightly sweet, tangy and bright, with a nice bite and a smoky aftertaste.

3½ pounds raspberries (about 14 cups)	4 dried chipotle peppers
2 cups water	1½ cups sugar

Combine the raspberries and water in a heavy-bottomed pot, set it over medium heat, and bring it to a gentle boil. Reduce the heat, and simmer, uncovered, stirring occasionally, until the fruit is very soft, about 10 minutes.

Place a colander lined with a clean towel or cheesecloth over a deep bowl. Add the fruit, and let it drip for at least 2 hours or overnight. Gather the ends of the towel together, and squeeze out the juice, scraping the underside of the cloth with a spoon. The juice may appear cloudy, but it will turn dark with the addition of the peppers. Discard the solids left in the towel.

Measure the juice. You should have about 5½ to 6 cups. For every 1 cup of juice, you will want ¼ cup of sugar; adjust the quantity of sugar accordingly.

Put the chipotles in a small bowl and cover them with boiling water. Soak the peppers until they are soft enough to handle, about 15 minutes. Remove the seeds and membranes from the peppers.

Combine the raspberry juice, chipotle peppers, and sugar in a 10-inch sauté pan, and stir to help dissolve the sugar. Measure the depth of the liquid using the dipstick method (page 9).

Set the pan over medium heat, bring the juice to a gentle boil, and then lower the heat. Simmer, uncovered, stirring occasionally and removing any foam that appears on the surface, until the liquid has reduced by a third to a half, about 20 to 30 minutes. Taste the syrup, and adjust the sugar level. Remove and discard the chipotle peppers.

Wash the jars, lids, and bands in very hot soapy water, rinse them well, and place them upside down on a clean towel to drain.

Pour the syrup into the jars. Wipe the rims with a clean wet cloth or paper towel, add the lids and bands, and finger tighten the bands.

Label the jars. Cool completely and tighten the bands before storing the jars in the refrigerator.

NOTE: If the syrup is too thick once it's cooled, return it to the pan, add a little water, and reheat. Pour the syrup back into the jars.

QUICK IDEAS // Surprisingly perfect over vanilla ice cream, the syrup is also great as a glaze for chicken. Whisk it into a salad dressing for sweetness and zip.

simple raspberry sauce

This sauce is so simple, so satisfying. It's equally good made with frozen fruit.

1½ pounds raspberries (about 6 cups)
 1 cup sugar
 ¼ cup lime juice

Put the raspberries, sugar, and lime juice into a 10-inch sauté pan, and stir to combine. Cover the pan, and macerate the fruit at room temperature for at least 2 hours or overnight.

Uncover the pan, set it over medium heat, and bring it to a gentle boil. Reduce the heat, and simmer, stirring occasionally, until the berries have cooked down into a sauce, about 5 to 7 minutes.

Wash the jars, lids, and bands in very hot soapy water, rinse them well, and place them upside down on a clean towel to drain.

Spoon the sauce into the jars, leaving a half inch of headroom to allow for expansion during freezing. Wipe the rims with a clean wet cloth or paper towel, add the lids and bands, and finger tighten the bands.

Label the jars. Cool completely and tighten the bands before storing the jars in the refrigerator or freezer.

QUICK IDEAS // This bright, intense, straightforward sauce is terrific on ice cream, swirled into yogurt, or spooned over pound cake. Whisk it into a simple vinaigrette; fold it into a fruit salad. Soak lady fingers in this sauce, and then slather them with whipped cream.

rhubarb

Last spring, when Mette visited family in Copenhagen, she brought back the seeds for the brilliant red rhubarb that grows abundantly in Danish backyards. To all of us in these northern parts, rhubarb heralds spring, an antidote sure to brighten up winter-weary plates. Nicknamed the pie plant, rhubarb is too often loaded with excess sugar and crust.

The best way to harvest rhubarb is to pull the stalks completely from the ground, including the curved foot, the sweetest part of the plant that's usually trimmed off and discarded.

vanilla-scented baked rhubarb compote

MAKES ABOUT 5 HALF-PINTS

Baked in the oven, the rhubarb pieces retain their shape as they become tender and silky. The vanilla is an elegant touch.

2 pounds rhubarb, cut into ½- to ¾-inch pieces (7 to 8 cups)

1 cup sugar

1 vanilla bean, split in half lengthwise

3 tablespoons lemon juice

Preheat the oven to 350 degrees. Place the rhubarb, sugar, vanilla bean, and lemon juice in a shallow, nonreactive, ovenproof dish large enough to hold the rhubarb in one layer and mix well. Place the pan on the middle rack, and bake, uncovered, until the liquid starts to thicken and the rhubarb looks slightly dry on top, about 40 minutes. Remove the pan from the oven. The compote will thicken as the rhubarb cools. Do not stir the compote, as the rhubarb pieces will fall apart. Discard the vanilla bean.

Wash the jars, lids, and bands in very hot soapy water, rinse them well, and place them upside down on a clean towel to drain.

Spoon the compote into the jars, leaving a half inch of headroom to allow for expansion during freezing. Wipe the rims with a clean wet cloth or paper towel, add the lids and bands, and finger tighten the bands.

Label the jars. Cool completely and tighten the bands before storing the jars in the refrigerator or freezer.

QUICK IDEAS // The vanilla in this compote makes it a perfect match for vanilla ice cream and yogurt. It's lovely served over sponge cake or angel food cake and topped with whipped cream.

mint and chili sweet pickled rhubarb

MAKES ABOUT 3 HALF-PINTS

The cookbook *Smag,* by Danish author Kille Enna, is innovative, contemporary, and totally Nordic. Its upbeat, boldly seasoned recipes are the inspiration for the cacophony of flavors—cool, hot, sweet, tangy—in Mette's pickled rhubarb. It brightens appetizers, salads, meats, and sides. Make this early in the season when the rhubarb is young and delicate. Note that the rhubarb's wide foot is the sweetest, juiciest, and most tender part of the stalk.

¾ pound rhubarb, cut diagonally into ¾-inch pieces (about 3 cups)

3 sprigs mint

6 wide bands lime zest

1 cup cider vinegar

½ cup sugar

2 teaspoons salt

1 teaspoon crushed red pepper flakes

Wash the jars, lids, and bands in very hot soapy water, rinse them well, and place them upside down on a clean towel to drain.

Divide the rhubarb among the jars. Place 1 sprig of mint and 2 bands of lime zest in each jar.

In a small saucepan, bring the vinegar, sugar, salt, and crushed red pepper flakes to a simmer. Cook, stirring to dissolve the sugar, about 3 to 4 minutes.

Divide the liquid among the jars. Cover each jar with a square of wax paper slightly larger than the jar opening, fold in the corners with a clean spoon, and push down gently so some of the brine comes up over the wax paper. Wipe the rims with a clean wet cloth or paper towel, add the lids and bands, and finger tighten the bands.

Label the jars. Cool completely and tighten the bands before storing the jars in the refrigerator.

QUICK IDEAS // Finely dice the pickled rhubarb, and toss it into salsa. Serve it over grilled pork or salmon. It pairs nicely with soft cheeses and cured meat.

roasted rhubarb ketchup

Rhubarb, technically a vegetable, works beautifully in this spicy sauce. The recipe is easily doubled.

2 pounds rhubarb, chopped into ½-inch pieces (about 8 cups)

1 cup medium-diced onions

1 tablespoon minced garlic

½ cup water

3 tablespoons cider vinegar

1 teaspoon crushed red pepper flakes

½ teaspoon celery seeds

½ teaspoon ground cumin

½ teaspoon ground coriander

½ teaspoon salt

Preheat the oven to 350 degrees. Combine the rhubarb, onion, garlic, and water in a medium nonreactive roasting pan. Cover the pan, and roast on the middle rack for 30 minutes. Uncover the pan, and continue roasting until the rhubarb is very tender, about 1 hour.

Place a medium mesh sieve over a deep bowl. Working in batches, press the rhubarb mixture through the sieve, scraping the underside of the sieve with a clean spoon. Discard the solids left in the sieve. Measure the sauce: you should have about 2 cups.

Turn the rhubarb sauce into a 10-inch sauté pan and stir in the vinegar, crushed red pepper flakes, celery seed, cumin, coriander, and salt. Bring to a gentle boil over medium heat; then reduce the heat. Simmer, uncovered, stirring, until the mixture is fairly thick, about 15 minutes.

Wash the jars, lids, and bands in very hot soapy water, rinse them well, and place them upside down on a clean towel to drain.

Spoon the ketchup into the jars, leaving a half inch of headroom to allow for expansion during freezing. Wipe the rims with a clean wet cloth or paper towel, add the lids and bands, and finger tighten the bands.

Label the jars. Cool completely and tighten the bands before storing the jars in the refrigerator or freezer. Let the rhubarb rest for a couple of weeks in the refrigerator to allow the flavors to marry.

QUICK IDEAS // French fries and sweet potato fries taste even better when dipped into rhubarb ketchup. Slather it onto turkey burgers. Whisk it into mayonnaise or yogurt for a dip.

strawberries

Do not overcook strawberries! These recipes treat the sweet, local gems with minimal heat so they taste just picked. We've found that too many traditional recipes cook the berries with too much sugar, producing a jam that tastes like boiled candy.

Tiny, local berries are the sweetest and most delicate. Seek them out!

hot and tangy strawberry jam

MAKES ABOUT 2 HALF-PINTS

A happy combination, this recipe calls for out-of-season frozen strawberries, cayenne pepper, and in-season grapefruit. When fresh strawberries come into the market, substitute limes or lemons for the grapefruit.

2 (10-ounce) bags whole frozen strawberries, cut into smaller pieces while frozen (about 5 cups)

¾ cup cane sugar

3 tablespoons fresh red grapefruit juice

1 tablespoon finely grated grapefruit zest

½ teaspoon cayenne pepper (optional)

Put a small plate in the freezer for the set test. Combine all of the ingredients in a 10-inch sauté pan. Cover the pan, and macerate the fruit at room temperature for at least 1 hour or until soft and completely thawed.

Uncover the pan, and set it over medium heat. Bring the jam to a gentle boil, and then reduce the heat. Simmer, stirring occasionally and smashing the berries with a fork, until the jam begins to thicken, about 12 to 15 minutes.

Remove the pan from the heat, and do a set test (page 10). If the jam isn't thick enough, return the pan to the heat for a few minutes, and then repeat the test.

Wash the jars, lids, and bands in very hot soapy water, rinse them well, and place them upside down on a clean towel to drain.

Spoon the jam into the jars, leaving a half inch of headroom to allow for expansion during freezing. Wipe the rims with a clean wet cloth or paper towel, add the lids and bands, and finger tighten the bands.

Label the jars. Cool completely and tighten the bands before storing the jars in the refrigerator or freezer.

QUICK IDEAS // Serve the jam on slices of lemon pound cake and scones. Whisk it into a vinaigrette for spinach salad.

baked strawberry preserves with ginger and lemon verbena

MAKES 3 TO 4 HALF-PINTS

The fresher and sweeter the berries, the less sugar you'll need for this preserve. We don't call for pectin, so the consistency is thinner than that of most preserves. But we like this preserve's clean, straightforward taste and the firm texture of the fruit. Baking the berries retains their shape, so they're perfect for garnishing cakes and tarts.

2 pounds small strawberries, cleaned and halved; large berries halved and thickly sliced (about 5 to 6 cups)	2½-inch piece ginger, peel intact, quartered lengthwise
½ cup sugar	2 sprigs lemon verbena
	2 tablespoons cider vinegar

Preheat the oven to 350 degrees. Place all of the ingredients in a shallow, ovenproof pan. Stir to gently fold in the sugar and aromatics. Place the uncovered pan on the middle rack and bake, occasionally stirring gently, until the strawberries release their liquid and the mixture begins to thicken, about 40 minutes. Remove from the oven, and discard the ginger and lemon verbena. The mixture will thicken as it cools.

Wash the jars, lids, and bands in very hot soapy water, rinse them well, and place them upside down on a clean towel to drain.

Spoon the preserves into the jars, leaving a half inch of headroom to allow for expansion during freezing. Wipe the rims with a clean wet cloth or paper towel, add the lids and bands, and finger tighten the bands.

Label the jars. Cool completely and tighten the bands before storing the jars in the refrigerator or freezer.

QUICK IDEAS // We find ourselves eating this preserve straight from the jar. You can also spoon it over cheesecake and angel food cake. It's terrific in strawberry shortcake and tarts.

seasonings

SALTY
AND
SWEET

ginger

In recent years, we've begun to see fresh ginger at the farmers market. It's mild and sweet–what a treat. When ginger is pickled, that sweetness is heightened by the tang of vinegar. The ginger plant is very pretty. Buy it whole, and steep the leaves in tea.

3-in-1 ginger

CANDIED GINGER, GINGER SYRUP, GINGER SUGAR

Choose very fresh ginger for these recipes. You want it to be moist and tender with thin, almost papery skin. Find lovely, local, fresh ginger at farmers markets and co-ops through the summer. Come winter, the best ginger comes from Hawaii.

candied ginger

MAKES 4 QUARTER-PINTS

½ pound fresh ginger, peeled (see note
   on page 172)
2⅓ cups sugar
2 cups water

Using your sharpest knife, slice the ginger crosswise into very thin rounds.

Combine 2 cups of the sugar and 2 cups of water in a medium saucepan. Bring the water to a gentle boil over medium heat, stirring to dissolve the sugar. Add the ginger slices, and lower the heat. Simmer, uncovered and stirring occasionally, until the syrup has thickened a little, about 40 minutes.

Remove the pan from the heat, and let the ginger marinate in the syrup for 30 minutes.

Place a fine mesh sieve over a deep bowl, and strain the ginger, making sure you've removed as much liquid as possible. Reserve the syrup in the bowl. (See Ginger Syrup on page 172.)

Line two baking sheets with parchment. Arrange the ginger pieces in a single layer on the parchment. Let the ginger dry for at least 8 hours or overnight. The ginger will still be sticky.

Pour the remaining ⅓ cup of sugar into a bowl, and add the ginger. Use your fingers or a spoon to coat the ginger all over with sugar. Reserve the sugar. (See Ginger Sugar on page 172.)

Wash the jars, lids, and bands in very hot soapy water, rinse them well, and place them upside down on a clean towel to drain. Thoroughly dry the jars, lids, and bands; then pack the ginger in the jars. Label the jars, and store them in the refrigerator.

QUICK IDEAS // Candied ginger is fabulous in cakes and cookies, on ice cream and sorbet. Dip it in chocolate; toss it into trail mix! Candied ginger is called for in Blackberry Preserves with Lime and Candied Ginger (page 104) and Black Currant Jam with Candied Ginger and Lemon Thyme (page 130).

bonus! ginger syrup

MAKES ABOUT 2 HALF-PINTS

Yes, this really is a two-for-one. No extra cooking, just extra syrup!

Wash the jars, lids, and bands in very hot soapy water, rinse them well, and place them upside down on a clean towel to drain.

Pour the reserved syrup from the Candied Ginger recipe (page 171) into the jars, leaving a half inch of headroom to allow for expansion during freezing. Wipe the rims with a clean wet cloth or paper towel, add the lids and bands, and tighten the bands. Label the jars, and store them in the refrigerator or freezer.

QUICK IDEAS // Drizzle ginger syrup over pound cake and vanilla ice cream; swirl it into coffee and tea. Whisk the syrup into dressing and whipped cream. Mix it with sparkling water for a refreshing drink; add a splash of your favorite spirit for a wicked cocktail.

bonus, bonus! ginger sugar

After you have sugared the ginger pieces for Candied Ginger (page 171), store the "ginger sugar" in a clean jar.

QUICK IDEAS // Sprinkle ginger sugar on cakes, cookies, tarts, and scones before baking! It's awesome on oatmeal.

NOTE: The easiest way to peel ginger is to first separate the ginger into lobes: find the natural divisions on the tubers and either break or cut them there. With a teaspoon held at an angle, scrape the skin off the ginger. Slice off any dried parts with a paring knife.

honey pickled ginger

MAKES 3 QUARTER-PINTS

Young, fresh ginger is essential in this recipe. Use a mandoline or a sharp knife with a very steady hand. The ginger must be cut very, very thin! This pickled ginger is less sweet and much fresher tasting than the commercial stuff.

¾ cup rice vinegar

3 tablespoons honey

2 cups water

1 cup peeled and very thinly sliced ginger (about 4 ounces) (see note on page 172)

Wash the jars, lids, and bands in very hot soapy water, rinse them well, and place them upside down on a clean towel to drain.

In a medium bowl, combine the vinegar and honey, stirring to dissolve the honey.

In a medium pot, bring the water to a boil. Blanch the ginger in the boiling water for exactly 2 minutes.

Drain the ginger, and add it to the vinegar mixture. Stir to mix well. Divide the ginger pieces among the jars, and then pour in the vinegar, leaving a half inch of headroom. Cover each jar with a square of wax paper slightly larger than the jar opening, fold in the corners with a clean spoon, and push down gently so some of the brine comes up over the wax paper. Wipe the rims with a clean wet cloth or paper towel, add the lids, and tighten the bands.

Label the jars, and store them in the refrigerator. The ginger tastes best if left to mature for a week before eating.

QUICK IDEAS // The traditional condiment for sushi, pickled ginger also livens up smoked meat, grilled fish, and stir-fries.

herbs

The fresh herbs in these recipes are interchangeable. Vary the herbs depending on the season, what's coming from your garden, and what you like best.

pesto: the simplest fresh sauce

Italian for "pounded," pesto is most often made with basil, but the term can apply to any combination of herbs pounded together with a mortar and pestle or whizzed in a food processor or blender. Following the basic proportions in the guidelines below, you can make a variety of pesto with any herb you choose. Just adjust the nuts, cheeses, and oils to taste.

The five standard ingredients—herbs, garlic, nuts, cheese, and oil—are pounded together with optional salt, pepper, and lemon juice.

Herbs: Basil, parsley, cilantro, chives, lovage, sorrel, mint, nasturtium, and garlic scapes, alone or in combination, make great pesto.

Garlic: Except in garlic scape pesto, garlic is essential.

Nuts: Choose pine nuts, walnuts, almonds, hazelnuts, pecans, pistachios, and sunflower seeds and pepitas (not technically nuts), raw or lightly toasted.

Cheese: Use a dry, firm cheese. While Parmesan from Italy is traditional, a good domestic Parmesan is great, as is pecorino, a sheep's milk cheese with a sharper flavor than Parmesan.

Oil: Olive oil is the most commonly used oil, but do try sunflower oil for a milder option. Walnut and hazelnut oils have a more distinct nutty flavor.

any herb pesto

MAKES 2 QUARTER-PINTS

Use these guidelines to create your own pesto. Feel free to double or triple the recipe because pesto freezes nicely. We are especially fond of parsley pesto.

2 cups well-packed fresh herbs (2 ounces)	¼ cup oil
¼ cup chopped nuts	½ teaspoon salt
¼ cup shredded cheese	10 to 15 grinds black pepper
1 garlic clove, or to taste	1 tablespoon lemon juice (optional)

Using a mortar and pestle, a food processor fitted with a steel blade, or a blender, process the herbs, nuts, cheese, and garlic. Slowly add the oil in a steady stream to make a thick paste. Season to taste with salt, pepper, and lemon juice (if using). Store the pesto in the refrigerator for up to 2 weeks or freeze it.

QUICK IDEAS // Quadruple the recipe, and spread the pesto in a ¼- to ½-inch layer on a 9 × 13-inch baking sheet lined with parchment. Pop the pan in the freezer for about 1 hour. Cut the frozen pesto into 16 squares (each square equals about ¼ cup), as shown in the picture. Place small pieces of parchment paper between the frozen pesto pieces, and put them in resealable bags to store in the freezer. The portioned-out pesto will be ready to toss into a soup or pasta or to season roast chicken.

minty mint syrup

MAKES ABOUT 3 HALF-PINTS

The bright flavor of this mint syrup derives its intensity from pounding the leaves to release the oils before they macerate with the rest of the ingredients. This recipe makes quick use of too much backyard mint. Use any varieties of mint you have on hand. The syrup freezes beautifully.

1½ cups packed mint leaves
    (about 1½ ounces)
 1 cup sugar

¼ cup lemon juice
2½ cups boiling water

Clean the mint leaves well. Dry them in a salad spinner, or layer them between clean towels, pressing gently to remove as much moisture as possible.

In a 10-inch sauté pan, stir together the mint leaves, sugar, and lemon juice. Using a muddler, a wooden spoon, or a fork, release the oils by pounding the leaves until the mint looks like cooked spinach. Cover the pan, and macerate the mint at room temperature for at least 1 hour. Add the boiling water to the sauté pan, cover, and macerate at room temperature for at least 6 hours or overnight.

Uncover the pan, set it over medium heat, and gently boil the mint mixture, stirring lightly, until the sugar dissolves.

Place a fine mesh sieve or a cloth-lined colander over a deep bowl, turn the mint into the sieve, and drain until liquid ceases dribbling from the sieve (do not press the mint), about 15 to 20 minutes. Discard the mint.

Wash the jars, lids, and bands in very hot soapy water, rinse them well, and place them upside down on a clean towel to drain.

Pour the syrup into the jars, leaving a half inch of headroom to allow for expansion during freezing. Wipe the rims with a clean wet cloth or paper towel, add the lids and bands, and finger tighten the bands.

Label the jars. Cool completely and tighten the bands before storing the jars in the refrigerator or freezer.

QUICK IDEAS // This bright fresh syrup perks up cocktails—mint juleps, vodka spritzers, and lemonade. Drizzle it over chocolate ice cream, brownies, and lemon sorbet.

traditional mint sauce

Don't limit this quick, easy sauce to lamb. It's sweet, tart, and refreshing and makes great use of an overabundance of backyard mint.

Be sure to use just the leaves, not the bitter stems, in this sauce. You can chop the leaves by hand or pulse them in a food processor, but do not overprocess.

- 1 cup champagne vinegar
- ⅓ cup sugar
- 4 cups packed clean mint leaves
   (about 4 ounces)
   pinch of sea salt

Combine the vinegar and sugar in a small saucepan. Bring it to a gentle boil, and stir to dissolve the sugar. Remove the pan from the heat, and allow the vinegar to cool completely, up to 2 hours (or put the pan in the freezer for about 30 minutes).

Boil a small amount of water; then set it aside to cool slightly.

Finely chop the mint by hand or in a food processor, adding a pinch of sugar to absorb the mint oil. Turn the chopped mint into a medium bowl, and pour the hot water over the mint.

Drain the mint through a fine mesh sieve, and then place it on paper towels and pat it dry. Return the mint to a dry bowl, and add a pinch of salt.

Wash the jars, lids, and bands in very hot soapy water, rinse them well, and place them upside down on a clean towel to drain.

Distribute the chopped, dry mint among the jars. Pour the cold vinegar over the mint, leaving a half inch of headroom to allow for expansion during freezing. Cover each jar with a square of wax paper slightly larger than the jar opening, fold in the corners with a clean spoon, and push down gently so some of the brine comes up over the wax paper. Wipe the rims with a clean wet cloth or paper towel, add the lids and bands, and tighten the bands. Label the jars, and store them in the refrigerator or freezer.

QUICK IDEAS // The classic partner to roast or grilled lamb, this sauce is equally wonderful on grilled eggplant, chicken tagine, or curry and as a garnish to hummus.

horseradish

Horseradish is the Nordic kitchen's equivalent of the hot chilies and ginger prevalent in warm-climate cuisines. This root can be tricky to handle. The fumes released as you grate the root can make you gasp and cause your eyes to sting—keep your head back as you work. Plan to grate the horseradish outside or be sure to open all the windows in the kitchen.

pickled horseradish

Timing is everything! For a mild condiment, add the vinegar right away. If you want more punch, wait up to 3 minutes before adding the vinegar. As soon as oxygen hits the root, it becomes hotter; vinegar stabilizes the hotness.

1	quart water	2	bay leaves
1½	teaspoons salt	1	teaspoon black peppercorns
1½	cups white wine vinegar	½	pound fresh horseradish

Wash the jars, lids, and bands in very hot soapy water, rinse them well, and place them upside down on a clean towel to drain.

In a medium pan, bring the water and salt almost to a boil. Stir to dissolve the salt, remove the pan from the heat, and set it aside.

In a medium saucepan, stir together the vinegar, bay leaves, and peppercorns. Bring the brine to a boil over high heat. Remove the pan from the heat, and let the brine rest.

When the salted water is cool enough to touch, peel the horseradish and place it in the water. Once all of the horseradish is peeled, coarsely grate the horseradish with a box grater or a food processor fitted with a grating disc. Return the grated horseradish to the salted water.

Drain the horseradish through a fine mesh sieve, pressing to squeeze out as much water as possible. Fill the jars with the grated horseradish.

Strain the brine, and add it to the jars, leaving a half inch of headroom to allow for expansion during freezing. Cover each jar with a square of wax paper slightly larger than the jar opening, fold in the corners with a clean spoon, and push down gently so some of the brine comes up over the wax paper. Wipe the rims with a clean wet cloth or paper towel, add the lids and bands, and tighten the bands. Label the jars, and store them in the refrigerator or freezer.

QUICK IDEAS // Make cocktail sauce for shrimp and seafood by stirring a few teaspoons of pickled horseradish into ketchup. To make Thousand Island dressing, stir a little pickled horseradish and ketchup into mayonnaise. To make the classic horseradish sauce for roast beef, stir a few teaspoons of pickled horseradish into sour cream. Use this horseradish in the Smoked Paprika and Horseradish Mustard (page 183).

mustard

Mustard plants grow like weeds and are beloved by honeybees. These recipes are super easy, but they do require a little patience. The seeds need to soak for at least one day, so plan ahead.

coarse-grain chili mustard

MAKES ABOUT 4 HALF-PINTS

This is an all-purpose mustard—not too hot, not too sweet. The recipe can easily be cut in half, but since mustard lasts indefinitely and makes a great gift, you might as well make the whole batch. The brown mustard seeds give the condiment a coarse stone-ground appearance.

⅔ cup yellow mustard seeds

½ cup brown mustard seeds

1½ cups Vinho Verde or other dry white wine

⅓ cup mustard powder

⅓ cup white wine vinegar

¼ cup packed light brown sugar

1 tablespoon crushed red pepper flakes

2 teaspoons salt

1 teaspoon ground turmeric

Put the yellow and the brown mustard seeds in a glass or stainless steel bowl, and pour in the Vinho Verde. Cover the bowl, and leave it at room temperature to let the seeds swell and soften, at least 1 day and up to 3 days.

Turn the soaked mustard seeds into a food processor fitted with a steel blade, and process, stopping to scrape down the sides, until the seeds are broken and the mixture appears creamy, about 1 minute. (Most of the brown mustard seeds will retain their shape while the yellow seeds will dissolve.)

Add the mustard powder, vinegar, light brown sugar, crushed red pepper flakes, salt, and turmeric to the food processor and run, scraping down the sides, until the mixture is relatively smooth and thick, about 2 minutes. If the mustard looks dry, add a little more wine or water, and run the food processor for a few more seconds to mix well.

Wash the jars, lids, and bands in very hot soapy water, rinse them well, and place them upside down on a clean towel to drain.

Fill the jars with the mustard. Wipe the rims with a clean wet cloth or paper towel, add the lids and bands, and tighten the bands. Label the jars.

Let the jars sit at room temperature for a week or longer before refrigerating them so the flavors mellow. Once the mustard is stored in the refrigerator, the flavors stabilize. If the mustard seems dry after you begin to use it, stir in a few drops of vinegar. Store the mustard in the refrigerator.

QUICK IDEAS // This is a bright, assertive mustard. Use it with strong meats and grilled sausages.

honey mustard

MAKES ABOUT 3 QUARTER-PINTS

Honey tames the flame here, making this mustard just right for Midwest sausages on the grill.

½ cup yellow mustard seeds	3 tablespoons honey
½ cup Vinho Verde or other dry white wine	1 teaspoon ground allspice
¼ cup white wine vinegar	1 teaspoon ground ginger

Put the mustard seeds in a glass or stainless steel bowl and pour in the Vinho Verde. Cover the bowl, and let it sit at room temperature so the seeds swell and soften, at least 1 day and up to 3 days.

Turn the soaked mustard seeds into a food processor fitted with a steel blade, and process the mixture for 1 or 2 minutes, scraping down the sides, until the seeds have broken and the mixture is creamy.

Add the vinegar, honey, allspice, and ginger, and process, scraping down the sides, until the mixture is thick and fairly smooth, about 2 minutes. If the mustard looks dry, add a little more wine or some water, and run the food processor for a few more seconds to mix well.

Wash the jars, lids, and bands in very hot soapy water, rinse them well, and place them upside down on a clean towel to drain.

Fill the jars with the mustard. Wipe the rims with a clean wet cloth or paper towel, add the lids and bands, and tighten the bands. Label the jars.

Let the jars sit at room temperature for a week or longer before refrigerating them so the flavors mellow. Once the mustard is stored in the refrigerator, the flavors stabilize. If the mustard seems dry after you begin to use it, stir in a few drops of vinegar. Store the mustard in the refrigerator.

QUICK IDEAS // This is *the* mustard for glazing a ham, brushing on pork chops as they come off the grill, and slathering on sandwiches.

smoked paprika and horseradish mustard

MAKES 2 TO 3 QUARTER-PINTS

Strong stuff, this mustard, smoky and hot all at once. The brown mustard seeds are spicier than the yellow seeds, and they tend to hold their shape. They give the mustard a nice grainy texture.

3 tablespoons yellow mustard seeds

2 tablespoons brown mustard seeds

⅓ cup rice vinegar

⅓ cup water

1 tablespoon maple syrup or honey

1 teaspoon smoked sweet paprika

1 tablespoon Pickled Horseradish (page 179) or prepared horseradish

1 teaspoon salt

Combine all of the ingredients in a glass or stainless steel bowl, and mix well. Cover the bowl, and let it sit at room temperature so the seeds swell and soften, at least 1 day and up to 3 days.

Turn the mixture into a food processor fitted with a steel blade, and process, scraping down the sides occasionally, until the mixture becomes thick, about 2 to 3 minutes. If the mustard appears dry, add a little more water, and run the food processor a few more seconds to mix well.

Wash the jars, lids, and bands in very hot soapy water, rinse them well, and place them upside down on a clean towel to drain.

Fill the jars with the mustard. Wipe the rims with a clean wet cloth or paper towel, add the lids and bands, and tighten the bands. Label the jars.

Let the jars sit at room temperature for a week or longer before refrigerating them so the flavors mellow. Once the mustard is stored in the refrigerator, the flavors stabilize. If the mustard seems dry after you begin to use it, stir in a few drops of vinegar. Store the mustard in the refrigerator.

QUICK IDEAS // Smoky and hot, this mustard is not for the tame of heart. Use it sparingly on bratwurst, roast pork, and smoked meat.

stout mustard

This is classic pub mustard, so use a nice dark beer from a good microbrewery. It's not as hot as English Colman's, but it does pack plenty of punch. Be sure to grind the brown mustard seeds in a spice grinder or a blender before soaking them; the food processor will not break them up later.

¾ cup brown mustard seeds, coarsely ground in a spice grinder or a blender	2 teaspoons ground coriander
1 cup stout or other dark, strong beer	1 teaspoon ground turmeric
2 tablespoons malt vinegar	1 teaspoon celery seeds
¼ cup mustard powder	1 teaspoon ground allspice
	1 teaspoon salt

Combine the mustard seeds and stout in a glass or stainless steel bowl. Cover the bowl, and let it sit at room temperature so the seeds swell and soften, at least 1 day and up to 3 days.

Put the soaked mustard seeds, vinegar, mustard powder, coriander, turmeric, celery seeds, allspice, and salt into a food processor fitted with a steel blade and process, stopping to scrape down the sides, into a paste, about 2 minutes. If the mustard looks dry, add a little more beer or water, and run the food processor for a few more seconds to mix well.

Wash the jars, lids, and bands in very hot soapy water, rinse them well, and place them upside down on a clean towel to drain.

Fill the jars with the mustard. Wipe the rims with a clean wet cloth or paper towel, add the lids and bands, and tighten the bands. Label the jars.

Let the jars sit at room temperature for a week or longer before refrigerating them so the flavors mellow. Once the mustard is stored in the refrigerator, the flavors stabilize. If the mustard seems dry after you begin to use it, stir in a few drops of vinegar. Store the mustard in the refrigerator.

QUICK IDEAS // This is the classic pub mustard—great on brats and sausages and alongside grilled meats.

nuts

Hazelnut, chestnut, black walnut, and hickory trees are important to our organic farmers. They provide a great wind block for the fields, help absorb water during the floods, retain topsoil, and return nutrients to the soil. These nuts are great fodder for animals and humans, and the oils are delicious too. The scrap wood from the trees makes a reliable biodiesel. Expect to see lots more nuts in the markets soon!

hazelnut chocolate spread

MAKES ABOUT 3 QUARTER-PINTS

Making your own hazelnut chocolate spread is a cinch. While we can't claim it's especially healthy, we know it contains less sugar and none of the emulsifiers, palm oil, and artificial flavors found in the commercial stuff. Midwest hazelnuts are becoming increasingly available throughout the region, and though they're smaller than those from the big West Coast and European growers, they pack a mighty good flavor. Choose cocoa power with a high fat content to make a very chocolaty spread.

½ pound hazelnuts (about 1¾ cups)

½ cup powdered sugar

⅓ cup cocoa powder

4 teaspoons sunflower oil, or more as needed

1 teaspoon vanilla extract

⅛ teaspoon salt

Preheat the oven to 375 degrees. Spread the hazelnuts in a single layer on a sheet pan, and put the pan on the oven's middle rack. Toast the nuts, shaking the pan occasionally, until they are fragrant and dark brown, about 10 to 15 minutes. Watch toward the end: the nuts go from dark to burned in no time!

When the nuts are cool enough to handle, turn batches of the nuts onto a clean dish towel, fold the towel over the nuts, and roll to loosen and remove most of the skins. Put the nuts into a food processor fitted with a steel blade and process, stopping to scrape down the sides, until you have a loose, thin paste, about 5 minutes.

Add the powdered sugar, cocoa powder, oil, vanilla, and salt, and process, stopping to scrape down the sides, until the spread is the consistency of peanut butter, about 2 minutes. If the spread seems dry, process in more oil a teaspoon at a time.

Wash the jars, lids, and bands in very hot soapy water, rinse them well, and place them upside down on a clean towel to drain.

Add hazelnut spread into the jars. Wipe the rims with a clean wet cloth or paper towel, add the lids and bands, and tighten the bands. Label the jars. Store the spread in the refrigerator. If the spread looks a little dry after storing it, stir in a small amount of sunflower oil to make it spreadable again.

QUICK IDEAS // Enjoy this rich, delicious spread straight from the jar. Slather it on croissants, sugar cookies, and pound cake.

maple pickled nuts

MAKES ABOUT 4 HALF-PINTS

These nuts are tangy-sweet and extremely versatile. Use your favorite nuts in this recipe.

1½ cups hazelnuts (about 6 ounces)
1½ cups whole blanched almonds (about
    6 ounces) (see note)
1 cup maple syrup

½ cup white balsamic vinegar
¼ cup fresh lemon juice
1 tablespoon finely grated lemon zest
2 sprigs rosemary

Preheat the oven to 375 degrees. Toast the almonds and hazelnuts on separate baking sheets until they begin to brown, turning the pans occasionally, about 10 to 12 minutes. Turn the hazelnuts onto a clean dish towel, fold the towel over the nuts, and roll to loosen and remove most of the skins. Turn the skinned hazelnuts into a bowl, and add the almonds.

In a medium saucepan, combine the maple syrup, vinegar, lemon juice, zest, and rosemary. Bring it to a gentle boil; then turn off the heat and let it rest for 15 minutes.

Wash the jars, lids, and bands in very hot soapy water, rinse them well, and place them upside down on a clean towel to drain.

Distribute the nuts among the jars. Strain the liquid into the jars through a fine mesh sieve. Discard the rosemary and zest left in the sieve.

Cover each jar with a square of wax paper slightly larger than the jar opening, fold in the corners with a clean spoon, and push down gently so some of the liquid comes up over the wax paper. This will help keep the nuts from floating up and out of the syrup.

Wipe the rims with a clean wet cloth or paper towel, add the lids and bands, and finger tighten the bands. Label the jars. Cool completely and tighten the bands before storing the jars in the refrigerator.

To allow the flavors to fully develop, let the nuts sit in the syrup for a few days before eating them.

NOTE: To blanch almonds, place the almonds in a small bowl and cover them with boiling water. After 1 minute, drain the almonds and refill the bowl with cold water. Using your fingers, gently squeeze off the skins and discard them. Place the skinned almonds on a dry towel.

QUICK IDEAS // These sweet savory nuts are great over ice cream, cakes, and shortbread. Serve them with a cheese plate. Toss them into a grain salad.

salt and sugar

Creating your own seasoned sugar and salt is quick and easy. These recipes make great use of garden herbs and bountiful citrus. Preserving herbs in salt helps draw the moisture from the herbs to extend their life. The key is to be sure the herbs are as fresh as possible.

Because you're blending to your own taste, you get the flavors you want. Keep these salts and sugars on hand for last-minute flourishes. They're brightly seasoned, so you'll find you use less sugar and salt and get more flavor! These make easy gifts. They travel well and need no refrigeration.

chive sea salt

MAKES ABOUT 3 QUARTER-PINTS

Chives are a classic Nordic seasoning. This chive salt will become a kitchen staple. The salt helps draw the moisture out of the chives while retaining that distinct, mild onion flavor. Early in the season, try adding a few pretty purple chive blossoms to the mix for an elegant touch.

½ cup chives or a mix of chives and chive flowers, completely dry and finely chopped

1 cup fine sea salt (see note)

Using your fingers, thoroughly mix together the chives and salt in a small bowl. Spread the salt mixture evenly over a large baking sheet, and let it dry for a day or so at room temperature (humidity will affect the amount of drying time required). The salt should no longer feel moist. Once it's dry, store the salt in very clean, dry jars.

NOTE: To make fine sea salt, place the salt in a blender or a spice grinder and run it for a few seconds.

QUICK IDEAS // Sprinkle this salt over roasted new potatoes, grilled steak, and roast chicken. Use it in a dry rub for turkey or pork. Used to season eggs and fish, it's straightforward, simple, and Nordic.

lemon chili sea salt

The chili will turn the salt to a lovely orange color, and the lemon adds a bright tang. The recipe will work with any thick-skinned citrus, so try using limes and grapefruit. This salt will last for months when stored in airtight containers at room temperature.

- ½ pound organic lemons
- 1 tablespoon crushed red pepper flakes
- ½ cup fine sea salt (see note)

Scrub the lemons well under running water, and pat them dry. Working with a vegetable peeler or very sharp knife, remove wide strips of zest from the fruit, being careful to avoid the white pith. To remove any pith from the zest, lay the peel on a cutting board and scrape off the pith with a sharp knife.

In a food processor fitted with a steel blade, pulse the zest, crushed red pepper flakes, and salt until the zest is ground fine, about 1 to 2 minutes. Scrape the sides of the food processor bowl between pulses. The salt may clump as the oil is released from the zest.

Turn the salt out on a baking sheet and spread it into a thin layer to dry for several hours or overnight (the drying time will vary, depending on the humidity).

Once the salt is dry, remove any clumps by pressing the salt through a medium mesh sieve. Store the salt in very clean, dry jars.

NOTE: To make fine sea salt, place the salt in a blender or a spice grinder and run it for a few seconds.

QUICK IDEAS // This salt is especially great on fish and chicken and wonderful sprinkled over roasted asparagus, carrots, and parsnips.

lime rosemary sugar

MAKES ABOUT 3 QUARTER-PINTS

Piney rosemary and tart lime make a terrific seasoning combo. We use this seasoned sugar with abandon! You can use any sugar for this, but we've found that cane sugar has more flavor.

⅓ to ½ pound organic limes
1 tablespoon rosemary leaves
1 cup cane sugar

Scrub the limes well under running water, and pat them dry. Working with a vegetable peeler or very sharp knife, remove wide strips of zest from the limes, being careful to avoid the white pith. To remove any pith from the zest, lay the peel on a cutting board and scrape off the pith with a sharp knife.

In a food processor fitted with a steel blade, pulse the zest, rosemary leaves, and sugar until the peel is ground fine, about 1 to 2 minutes, scraping the sides down between pulses. The sugar may clump as the oil is released from the zest.

Turn the sugar out on a baking sheet, and spread it into a thin layer to dry for several hours (drying time will vary, depending on the humidity).

Once the sugar is dry, remove any clumps by pressing it through a medium mesh sieve. Store the sugar in clean, dry jars.

QUICK IDEAS // Sprinkle this lime-kissed sugar over fresh fruit salad, cookies, cupcakes, pancakes, waffles, pound cake, and iced mint tea.

lavender–lemon thyme sugar

MAKES 3 QUARTER-PINTS

Use fresh lavender for the most intensely fragrant results. To keep the sugar from clumping, make sure the lavender flowers are thoroughly dry before mixing them with the sugar. Otherwise, use dried culinary lavender. It's available in the spice section of most co-ops and cooking stores, and also online. We prefer cane sugar here because of its coarser texture and light molasses note.

Lemon thyme is a fragrant, mellow variety of thyme. If it's not available, omit the thyme, increase the amount of lavender to taste, and add a little lemon zest. Regular thyme is simply too strong and will overpower the flavor of the lavender.

1 tablespoon lemon thyme leaves
6 tablespoons fresh lavender flowers, well
    rinsed and dried, or 2 tablespoons dried
1 cup cane sugar

In a small bowl, combine the lemon thyme and the lavender. With your thumb and index finger, work the herbs and flowers together to release their oils. They'll begin to clump, which is a good sign they're releasing their oils. Add the sugar, and work it in with your fingers until it is well mixed.

Spread the sugar evenly on a large baking sheet to dry at room temperature for a day or more, depending on the humidity. The sugar should no longer feel moist. Pack the sugar into clean, dry jars.

QUICK IDEAS // Sprinkle the seasoned sugar over frosted cupcakes, on fresh fruit, and over berry or apple tarts. It's terrific on waffles and pancakes too.

dukka

Dukka is a traditional Egyptian spice blend (some versions include herbs) most often mixed with olive oil as a dip for flatbread. There are as many recipes as there are families. This recipe is ours.

1¼ cups cooked or canned garbanzo beans, rinsed and patted dry (see note on page 194)

1 tablespoon olive oil

½ cup hazelnuts (about 2 ounces)

1½ tablespoons cumin seeds

2 tablespoons coriander seeds

1 teaspoon black peppercorns

½ cup black sesame seeds or white sesame seeds

1½ teaspoons salt

1 teaspoon sweet paprika

1 teaspoon cayenne pepper (optional)

Preheat the oven to 400 degrees. Place a baking sheet on the middle rack as the oven heats up. Toss the garbanzo beans with the olive oil in a small bowl. Place them in a single layer on the heated baking sheet. Toast the garbanzos, occasionally shaking the pan, until they are golden brown, about 30 to 40 minutes.

Place the hazelnuts on a separate baking sheet on the rack below the garbanzo beans, and toast them, shaking the pan occasionally, until their skins begin to crack, about 10 to 12 minutes.

Place the warm hazelnuts on a clean kitchen towel on the counter. Fold the towel over, and roll the nuts hard with your hands. The skins will start to loosen and come off.

Watching that they do not burn, toast the cumin seeds, coriander seeds, and peppercorns in a dry skillet set over low-medium heat just until fragrant, about 1 to 2 minutes. Turn the spices into a bowl, and set it aside.

Turn the sesame seeds into the skillet, and toast them for a couple of minutes. Set them aside in another small bowl.

Grind the toasted spices with a spice grinder or a mortar and pestle. Alternatively, place the spices in a resealable plastic bag, and crush them with a bottle, rolling pin, or empty canning jar. (It is easier to do this when the spices are still warm and brittle.)

In a food processor fitted with a steel blade, pulse the garbanzo beans until ground, and turn them into a large bowl. Then pulse the hazelnuts until ground, and add them to the ground garbanzo beans. Stir in the toasted whole sesame seeds, ground spices, salt, paprika, and cayenne pepper (if using).

continued on next page

Cool the mix completely before storing it in very clean, dry jars. Store the dukka in a cool, dark place.

NOTE: Use cooked or canned garbanzo beans in this recipe. A 15 ½-ounce can provides about 1¼ cups. Rinse the garbanzos well, and dry them gently in a towel. With your fingers, slip off the cloudy coating around each bean. This gives the beans a much cleaner flavor.

QUICK IDEAS // Sprinkle dukka on top of roasted vegetables and soup. Mix it in with cooked rice. It's great sprinkled over chèvre or any fresh soft cheese, hummus, and roasted or grilled meat and chicken for a spicy, nutty crunch.

acknowledgments

All books, especially cookbooks, are collaborations, but this work is also a tribute to longstanding friendships and shared vision and values. We are grateful for the engagement and encouragement of our many friends and our families. Our deepest thanks to . . .

The crackerjack team at the University of Minnesota Press: our editor, Erik Anderson, for his warmth, good humor, guidance, and thoughtful attention to this project; Kristian Tvedten, for his skill and patience tracking all the details; Brian Donahue, for his judgment and design savvy; and Pam Price, copy editor, beekeeper, gardener, for her keen eye and wit.

Mette's son Alexander Watchman and daughter-in-law Abby Weber, for their inspiration and ideas; Robin Krause, for teaching Mette to be a fearless cook; Georgina Frankel and Martha Coventry (the Washingtons), for tasting and testing; Pipper Berg Madsen and Jeff Hardwick, for being adventurous eaters; Haydn Wyckoff, for coining the term *condiMettes*; Maj-Britt Riget, for sharing her knowledge of Danish cookbooks and food trends and escorting Mette to foodie haunts in Denmark; Beth's husband, Kevin, and their sons, Matt, Kip, and Tim, for their enthusiasm and pride in our endeavors.

Finally, thanks to all the farmers, gardeners, chefs, foragers, and cooks who contributed ideas, recipes, ingredients, and insights to this joyful book.

index

TIMOTHY DOOLEY

Beth Dooley has written several award-winning cookbooks, including *Savoring the Seasons of the Northern Heartland*, coauthored with Lucia Watson, a James Beard Award nominee; *The Northern Heartland Kitchen*; and *Minnesota's Bounty: The Farmers Market Cookbook*, all published by the University of Minnesota Press. She is also the author of *In Winter's Kitchen: Growing Roots and Breaking Bread in the Northern Heartland* and appears regularly on KARE 11 TV in the Twin Cities and on Minnesota Public Radio's "Appetites."

Mette Nielsen is a talented master gardener and photographer. She created the edible garden for the Birchwood Cafe in Minneapolis and partnered with Beth Dooley on *The Birchwood Cafe Cookbook* and *Minnesota's Bounty: The Farmers Market Cookbook*.

notes

notes

notes

notes

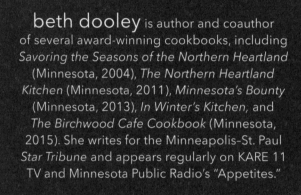

beth dooley is author and coauthor of several award-winning cookbooks, including *Savoring the Seasons of the Northern Heartland* (Minnesota, 2004), *The Northern Heartland Kitchen* (Minnesota, 2011), *Minnesota's Bounty* (Minnesota, 2013), *In Winter's Kitchen,* and *The Birchwood Cafe Cookbook* (Minnesota, 2015). She writes for the Minneapolis–St. Paul *Star Tribune* and appears regularly on KARE 11 TV and Minnesota Public Radio's "Appetites."

....

mette nielsen's photographs have been featured in numerous books, newspapers, and magazines. A talented master gardener, she created the edible garden for the Birchwood Cafe in Minneapolis and collaborated on *The Birchwood Cafe Cookbook* and *Minnesota's Bounty*.